GRADES
1

DAILY Word Ladders

80+ Word Study Activities That Target Key Phonics Skills to Boost Young Learners' Reading, Writing & Spelling Confidence

by Timothy V. Rasinski

New York ○ Toronto ○ London ○ Auckland ○ Sydney
New Delhi ○ Mexico City ○ Hong Kong ○ Buenos Aires

Teaching Resources

To all teachers and children who
take delight in words,

Make word study a game and
students will learn words!

Editor: Maria L. Chang
Designer: Grafica Inc.
Illustrations: Teresa Anderko

ISBN: 978-0-545-22379-9
Printed in the U.S.A.

15   40   20

Contents

The Ladders

Contents

Welcome to Word Ladders!

In this book you'll find more than 80 mini-word-study lessons that are also kid-pleasing games! To complete each Word Ladder takes less than ten minutes. However, each Word Ladder actively involves learners in analyzing the structure and meaning of words. To play, children begin with one word and then make a series of new words by changing or rearranging the letters in the previous word. With regular use, Word Ladders can go a long way toward developing your students' decoding and vocabulary skills.

How do Word Ladders work?

Let's say our first Word Ladder begins with the word *web*. The directions will tell children to change one letter in *web* to make a word that means "not dry." The word children will make, of course, is *wet*. The directions for the next word will then ask children to make a change in *wet* to form another word—perhaps *pet* or *set*. Children will form new words as they work up the ladder until they reach the top rung. If children get stuck on a rung along the way, they can come back to it, because the words before and after will give them the clues they need to figure out the word. Of course, you can also provide additional clues to help them figure out difficult words.

How do Word Ladders benefit children?

Word Ladders are great for building children's decoding, phonics, spelling, and vocabulary skills. When children add, take away, or rearrange letters to make a new word from one they have just made, they must examine sound-symbol relationships closely. This is just the kind of analysis that all children need to do in order to learn how to decode and spell accurately. And when the Ladder adds a bit of meaning in the form of a definition (for example, "what you make when you sit down"), it helps extend children's understanding of words and concepts. All of these skills are key to children's success in learning to read and write. So even though Word Ladders will feel like a game, children will be practicing essential literacy skills at the same time!

How do I teach a Word Ladder lesson?

Word Ladders are incredibly easy and quick to implement. Here are four simple steps:

1. Choose a Word Ladder to try. Each word ladder teaches a particular phonics lesson, like short-*a* words or *r*-controlled vowels.
2. Make a copy of the Word Ladder for each child.
3. Choose whether you want to do the Word Ladder with the class as a whole, or have children work alone, in pairs, or in groups. If children are emergent readers, you might read the clues to them and use a think-aloud method to model how to complete the activity. In addition, you might display a copy on an overhead projector to demonstrate how to fill in the word on each rung. As their skills develop, children can begin doing the Word Ladders independently.

4. At each new word, children will see two clues: the changes they need to make to the previous word ("change the first letter," "add a letter to the end," and so on), and a definition of or clue to the meaning of the word. Sometimes this clue will be a sentence in which the word is used in context but is left out for children to fill in. Move from word to word in this way, up the whole Word Ladder. Feel free to add clues if the word is challenging—letter position of the change; other sentence clues; or just tell students the word.

That's the lesson in a nutshell! It should take no longer than ten minutes to do. Once you're done, you might extend the lessons by having children sort the words into various categories. This can help them deepen their understanding and use of the words. For instance, you could sort them into:

- Grammatical categories (Which words are action words? Which words name people, animals, places, or things?)
- Word structure (Which words end with a silent *e*? Which words contain a consonant blend?)
- Word meaning (Which words express what a person can do or feel? Which do not?)

Additionally, you can create your own Word Ladders using copies of the blank puzzles on pages 90–93. Or you might invite children to make their own puzzles to exchange with classmates.

Tips for Working With Word Ladders

Try these tips to give children extra help in doing Word Ladders.

- List all the "answers" for the ladder (that is, the words for each rung) in random order on the board. Have children choose words from the list to complete the puzzle.

- Add your own clues to give children extra help as they work through each rung of a ladder. A recent event in your classroom or community could even inspire clues for words.

- If children are stuck on a particular rung, you might simply say the word aloud and see if children can spell it correctly by making appropriate changes in the previous word. Elaborate on the meanings of the words as children move their way up the ladder.

- Challenge children to come up with alternative definitions for the same words. Many words, like *bat*, *pet*, *bill*, and *lot*, have multiple meanings.

- Once children complete a ladder, add the words to a word wall. Encourage children to use the words in their speaking and writing.

Name _____

Read the clues. Then write the words.
Start at the bottom and climb to the top.

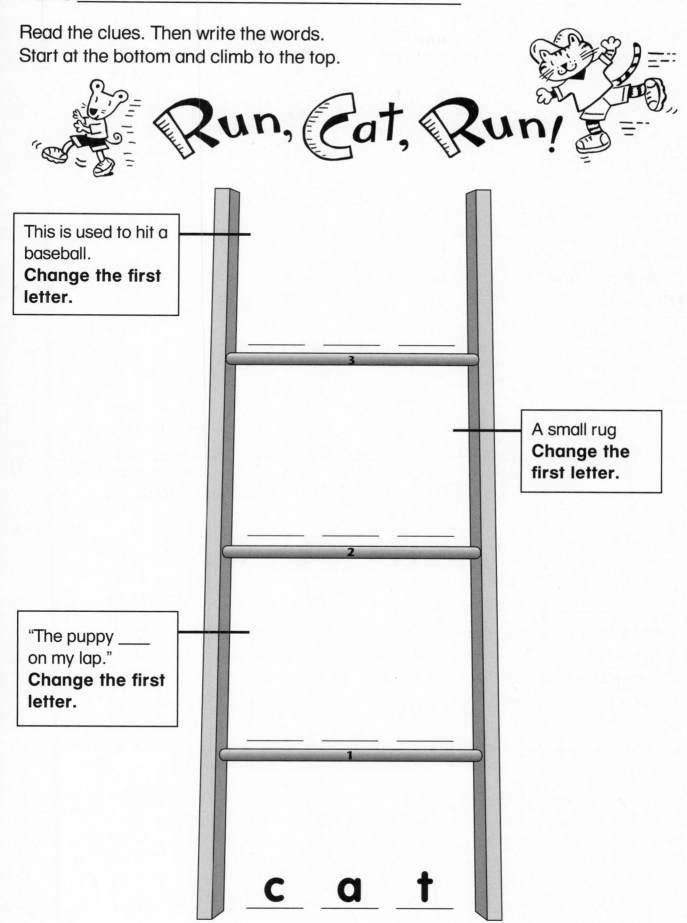

Run, Cat, Run!

This is used to hit a baseball.
Change the first letter.

3 _____

A small rug
Change the first letter.

2 _____

"The puppy ____ on my lap."
Change the first letter.

1 _____

c   a   t

Name _____

Read the clues. Then write the words.
Start at the bottom and climb to the top.

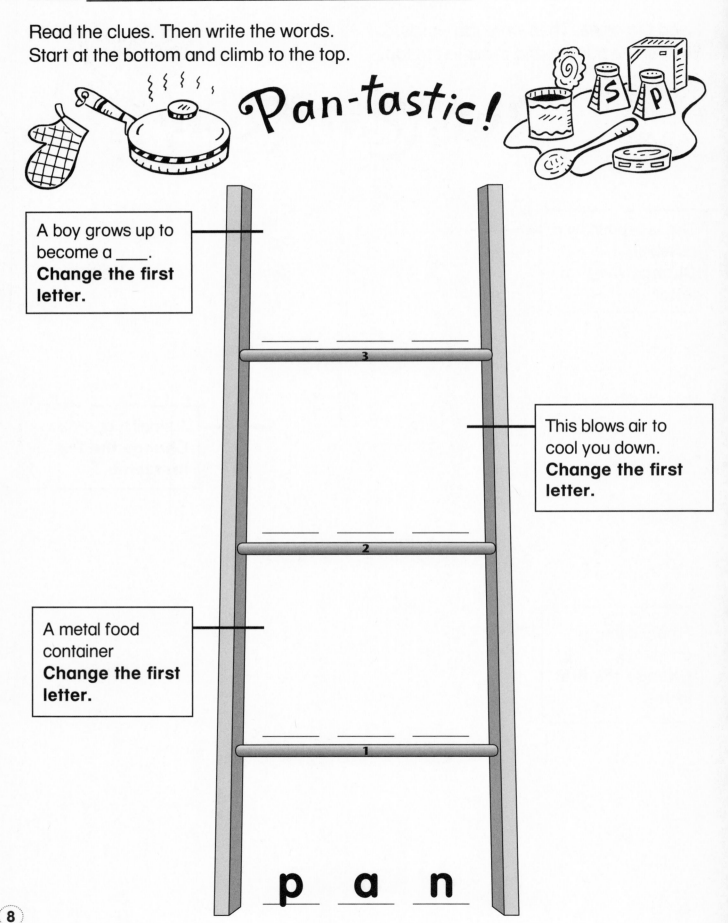

Pan-tastic!

A boy grows up to become a ___.
Change the first letter.

This blows air to cool you down.
Change the first letter.

A metal food container
Change the first letter.

3

2

1

p a n

8

Name _____

Read the clues. Then write the words.
Start at the bottom and climb to the top.

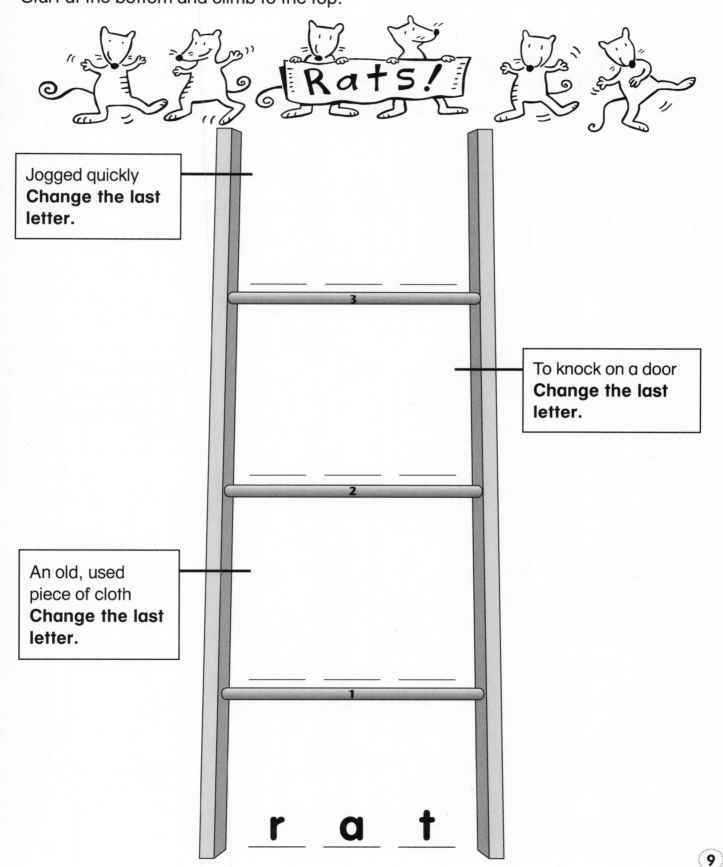

Jogged quickly
Change the last letter.

To knock on a door
Change the last letter.

An old, used piece of cloth
Change the last letter.

3

2

1

r   a   t

Name _____

Read the clues. Then write the words.
Start at the bottom and climb to the top.

Something soft,
like a cushion
**Change the last
letter.**

Where you fry
something
**Change the last
letter.**

A friend
**Change the last
letter.**

3

2

1

p   a   t

Name _____

Read the clues. Then write the words.
Start at the bottom and climb to the top.

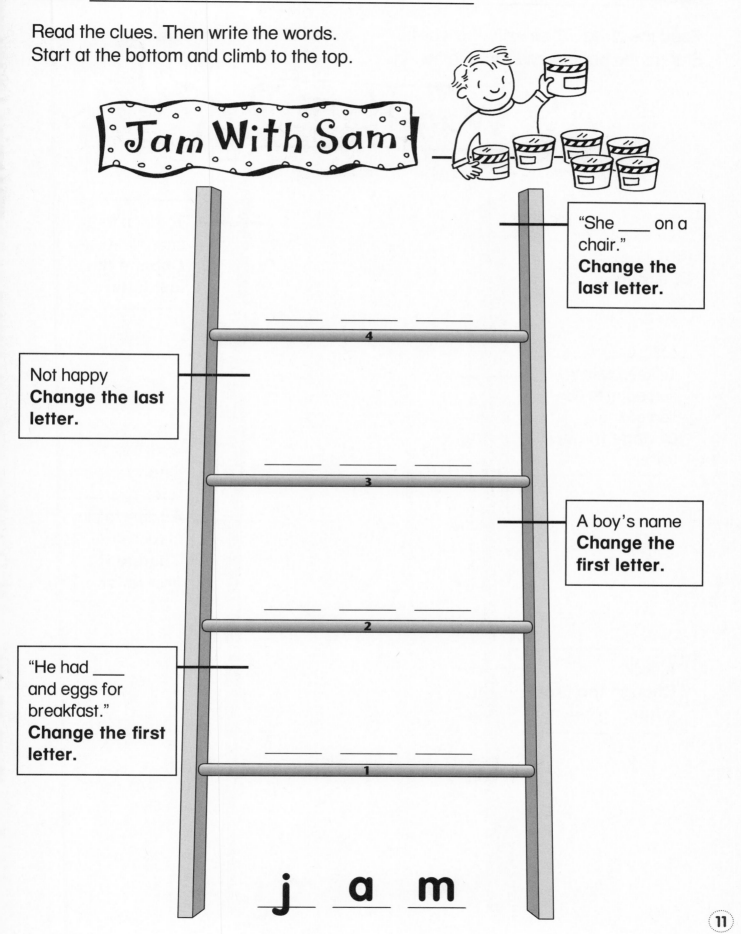

Jam With Sam

"She ___ on a chair."
Change the last letter.

Not happy
Change the last letter.

4 _____

A boy's name
Change the first letter.

3 _____

"He had ___ and eggs for breakfast."
Change the first letter.

2 _____

1 _____

j a m

Name _____

Read the clues. Then write the words.
Start at the bottom and climb to the top.

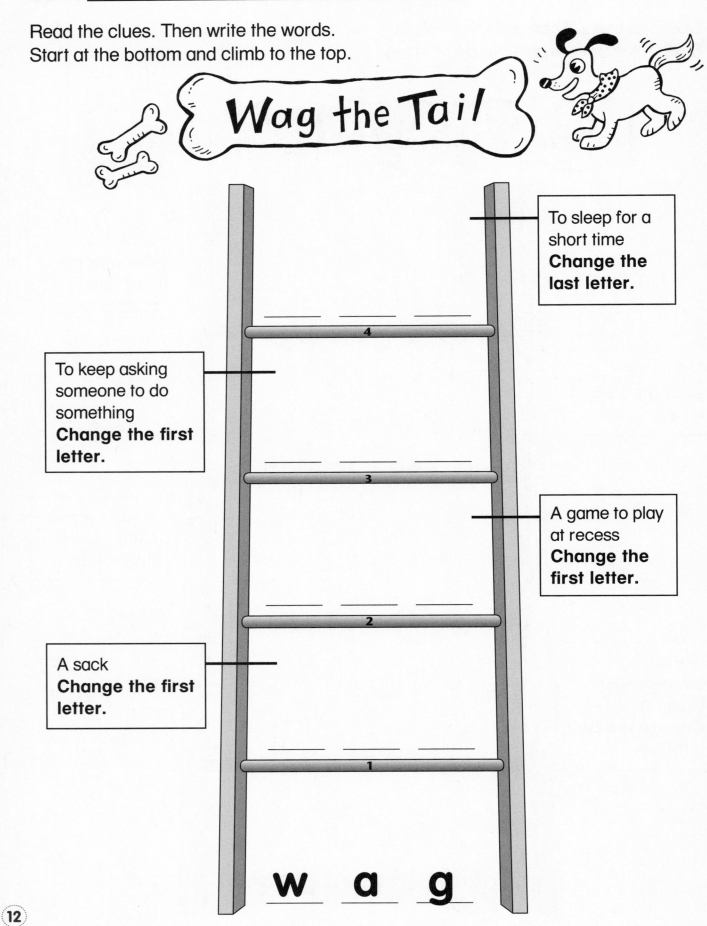

Wag the Tail

To sleep for a short time
Change the last letter.

To keep asking someone to do something
Change the first letter.

A game to play at recess
Change the first letter.

A sack
Change the first letter.

4

3

2

1

w a g

Name _____

Read the clues. Then write the words.
Start at the bottom and climb to the top.

Everybody Clap Your Hands!

A metal container for storing food **Change the last letter.**

A taxi **Change the last letter.**

A kind of hat **Change the first letter.**

To touch lightly **Change the first letter.**

What you make when you sit down **Take away the first letter.**

5

4

3

2

1

c l a p

Name _____

Read the clues. Then write the words.
Start at the bottom and climb to the top.

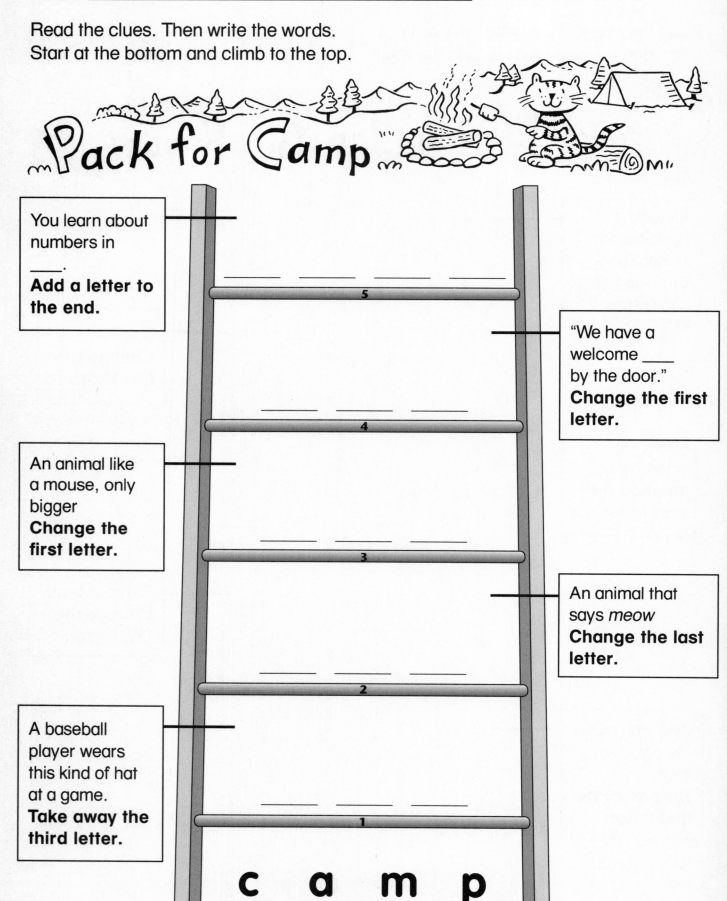

Pack for Camp

You learn about numbers in ____.
Add a letter to the end.

"We have a welcome ____ by the door."
Change the first letter.

An animal like a mouse, only bigger
Change the first letter.

An animal that says *meow*
Change the last letter.

A baseball player wears this kind of hat at a game.
Take away the third letter.

5

4

3

2

1

c a m p

Name _____

Read the clues. Then write the words.
Start at the bottom and climb to the top.

Jet Set

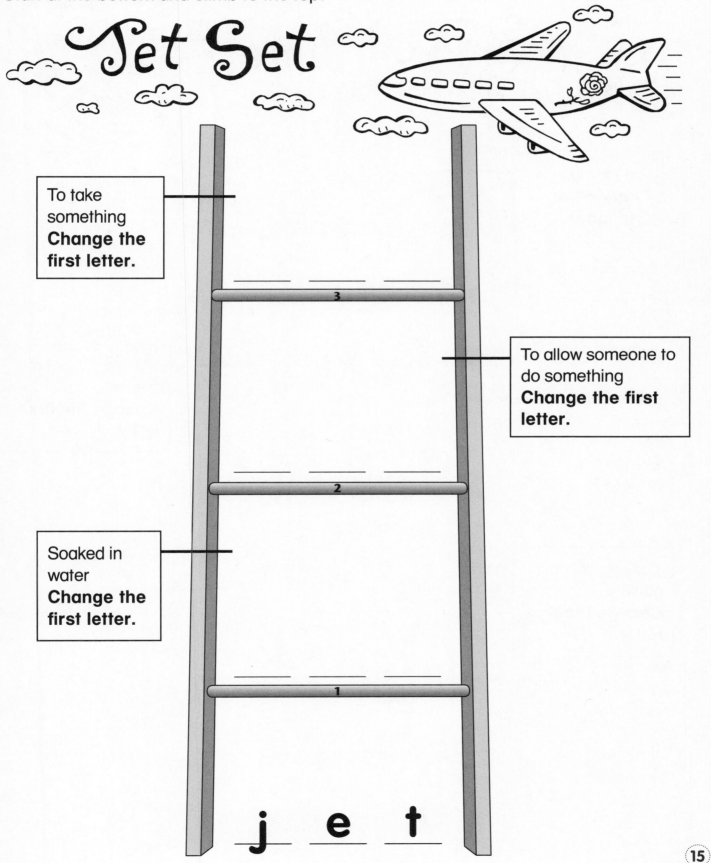

To take something **Change the first letter.**

To allow someone to do something **Change the first letter.**

Soaked in water **Change the first letter.**

Name _____

Read the clues. Then write the words.
Start at the bottom and climb to the top.

Bed Time

Get married
Change the first letter.

3

Walked in front of the line
Change the first letter.

2

The color of an apple
Change the first letter.

1

b   e   d

Name _____

Read the clues. Then write the words.
Start at the bottom and climb to the top.

Pen Pals

Lots of energy
Change the last letter.

3 _ _ _ _ _ _

A small piece of wood for hanging your coat
Change the last letter.

2 _ _ _ _ _ _

Your cat or dog
Change the last letter.

1 _ _ _ _ _ _

p e n

17

Name _____

Read the clues. Then write the words.
Start at the bottom and climb to the top.

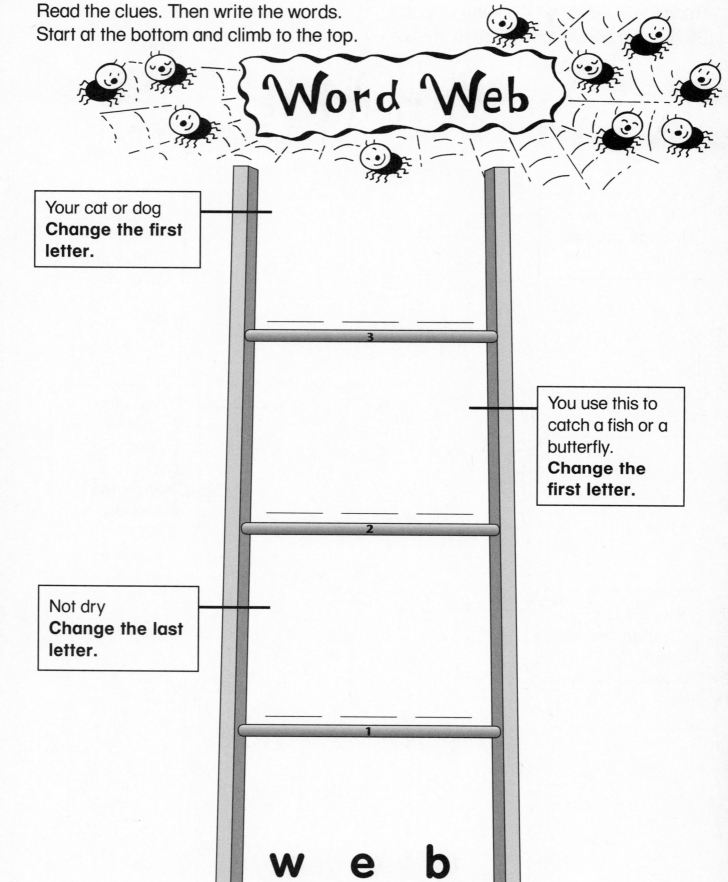

Word Web

Your cat or dog
Change the first letter.

You use this to catch a fish or a butterfly. **Change the first letter.**

Not dry
Change the last letter.

3

2

1

w e b

Name _____

Read the clues. Then write the words.
Start at the bottom and climb to the top.

On the Set

Where a bear
or fox might
sleep
**Change the
first letter.**

_____ _____ _____
4

Boys grow up to
become ____.
**Change the
last letter.**

_____ _____ _____
3

"I ____ my
friend after
school."
**Change the
first letter.**

_____ _____ _____
2

Opposite of *dry*
**Change the first
letter.**

_____ _____ _____
1

s   e   t

19

Name _____

Read the clues. Then write the words.
Start at the bottom and climb to the top.

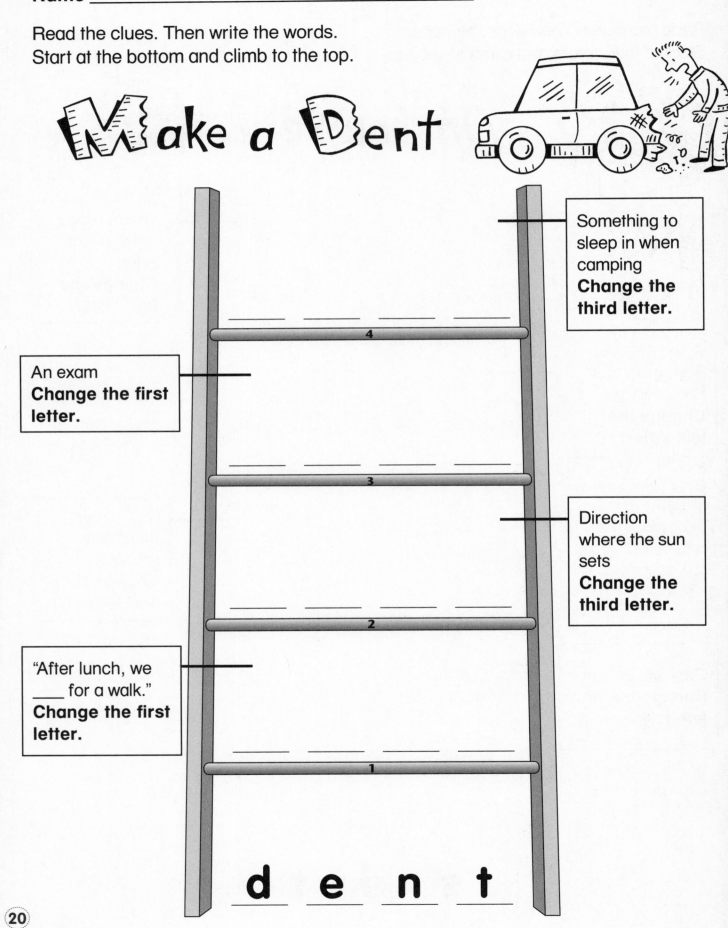

Make a Dent

Something to
sleep in when
camping
**Change the
third letter.**

4

An exam
**Change the first
letter.**

3

Direction
where the sun
sets
**Change the
third letter.**

2

"After lunch, we
____ for a walk."
**Change the first
letter.**

1

d e n t

20

Name _____

Read the clues. Then write the words.
Start at the bottom and climb to the top.

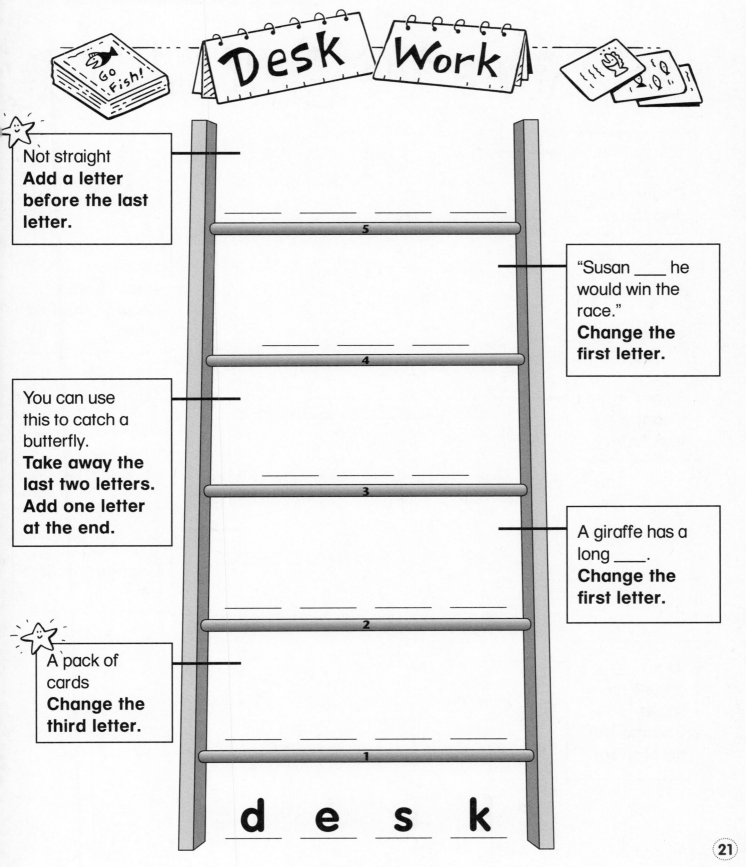

Not straight
Add a letter before the last letter.

"Susan ____ he would win the race."
Change the first letter.

You can use this to catch a butterfly.
Take away the last two letters. Add one letter at the end.

A giraffe has a long ____.
Change the first letter.

A pack of cards
Change the third letter.

d   e   s   k

Name _____

Read the clues. Then write the words.
Start at the bottom and climb to the top.

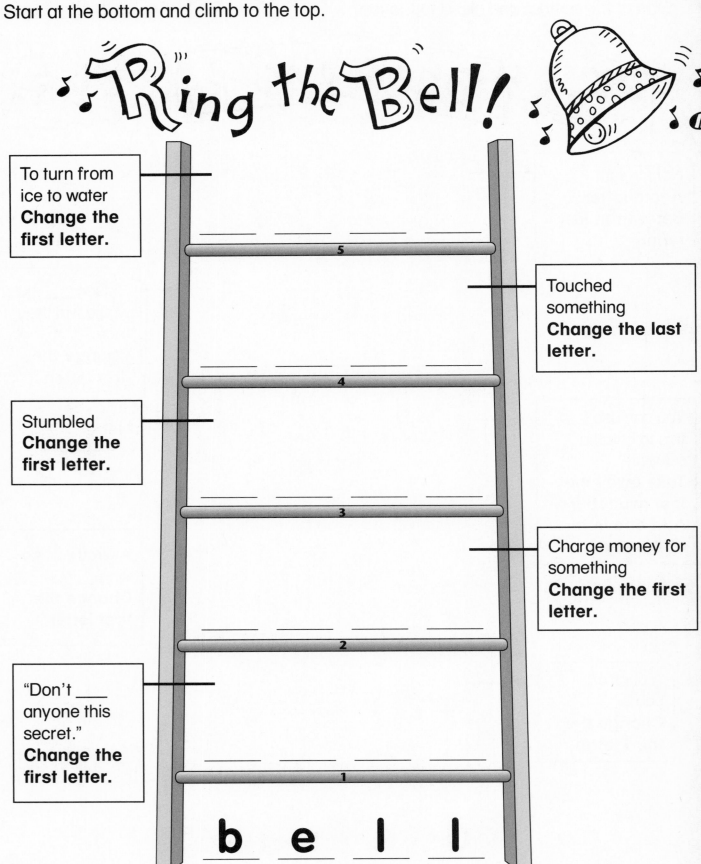

Ring the Bell!

To turn from ice to water **Change the first letter.**

Touched something **Change the last letter.**

Stumbled **Change the first letter.**

Charge money for something **Change the first letter.**

"Don't ____ anyone this secret." **Change the first letter.**

5

4

3

2

1

b e l l

Name _____

Read the clues. Then write the words.
Start at the bottom and climb to the top.

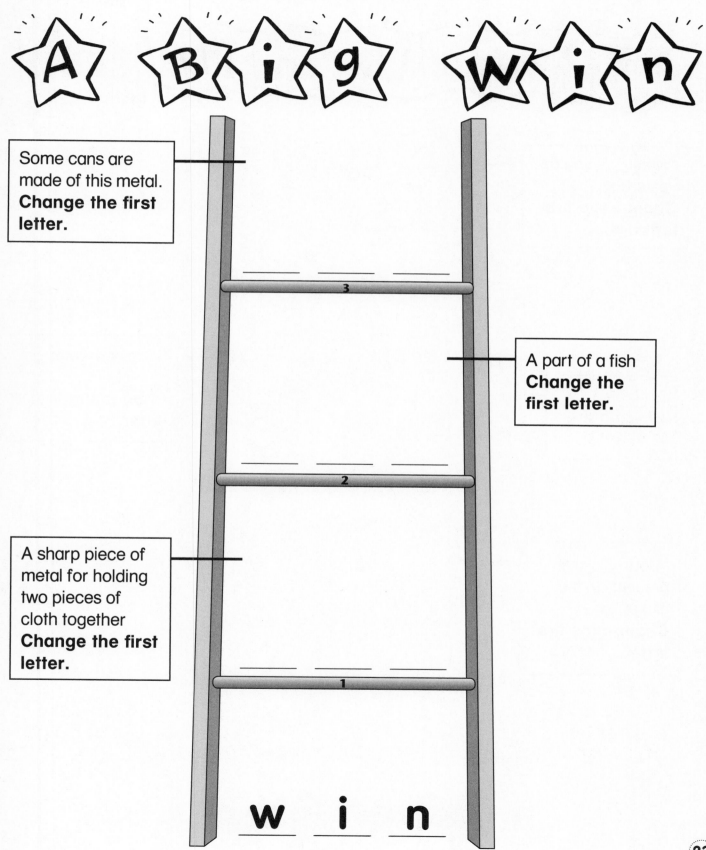

A Big Win

Some cans are made of this metal. **Change the first letter.**

A part of a fish **Change the first letter.**

A sharp piece of metal for holding two pieces of cloth together **Change the first letter.**

3

2

1

w i n

Name _____

Read the clues. Then write the words.
Start at the bottom and climb to the top.

Put a Lid on It!

"What ____ you do yesterday?"
Change the first letter.

Soap and water get ____ of dirt.
Change the first letter.

"Mom ____ our presents in the closet."
Change the first letter.

3

2

1

l i d

24

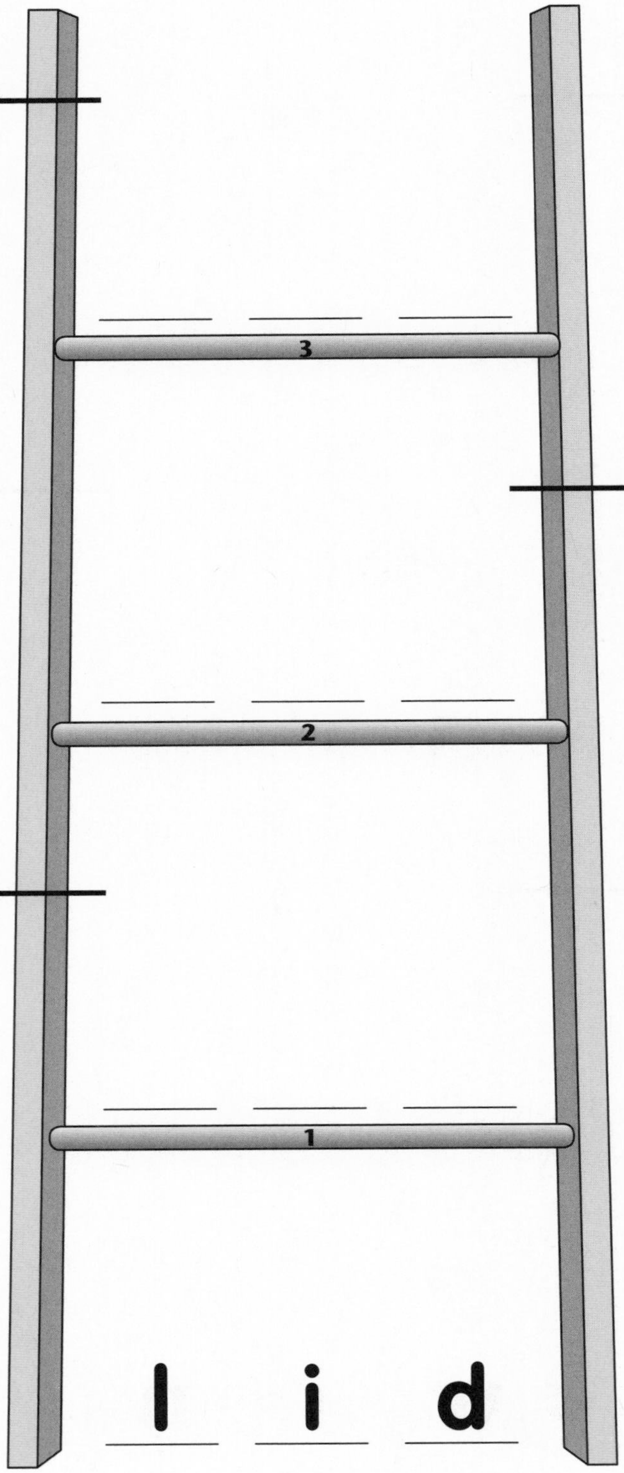

Name _____

Read the clues. Then write the words.
Start at the bottom and climb to the top.

The scared dog
____ under the
chair.
**Change the last
letter.**

That boy
**Change the
last letter.**

3

The bone above
your legs
**Change the last
letter.**

2

h   i   t

1

25

Name _____

Read the clues. Then write the words.
Start at the bottom and climb to the top.

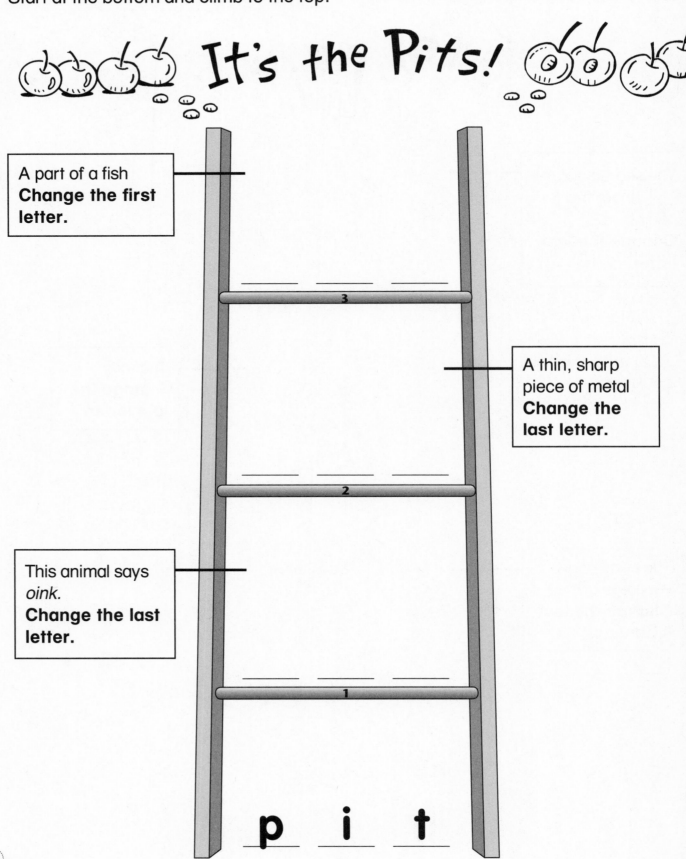

It's the Pits!

A part of a fish
Change the first letter.

A thin, sharp piece of metal
Change the last letter.

3

2

This animal says *oink.*
Change the last letter.

1

p i t

26

Name _____

Read the clues. Then write the words.
Start at the bottom and climb to the top.

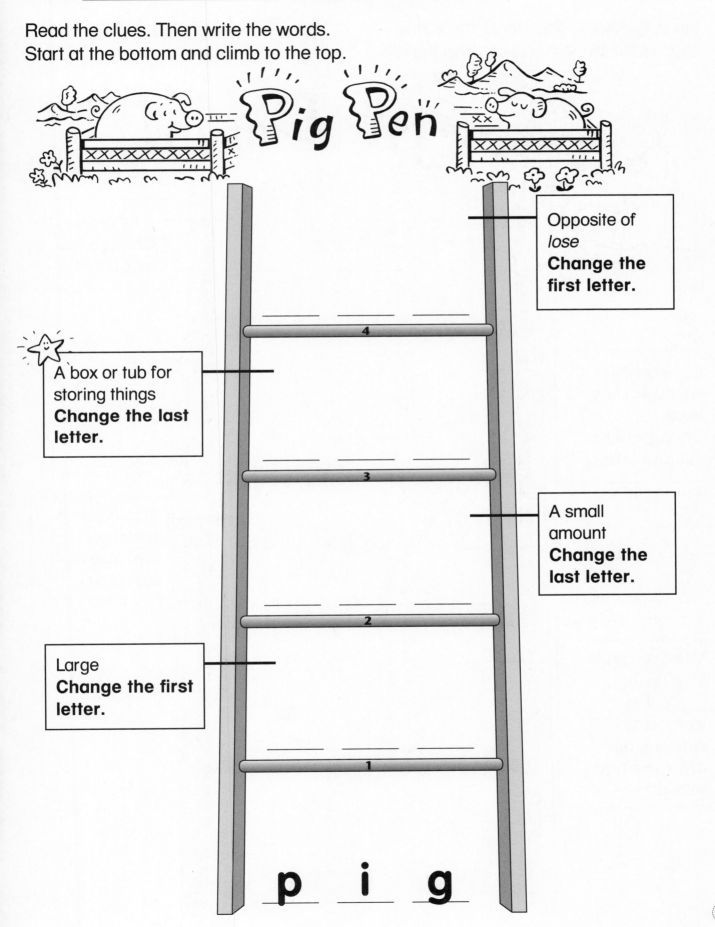

Opposite of *lose*
Change the first letter.

A box or tub for storing things
Change the last letter.

A small amount
Change the last letter.

Large
Change the first letter.

4

3

2

1

p   i   g

Name _____

Read the clues. Then write the words.
Start at the bottom and climb to the top.

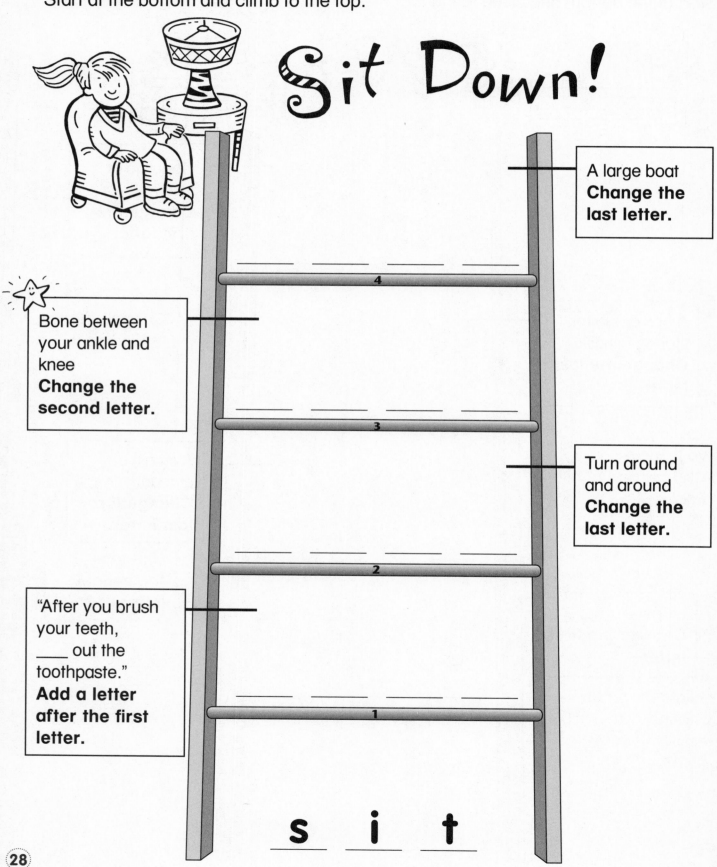

Sit Down!

A large boat
Change the last letter.

4 _____

Bone between your ankle and knee
Change the second letter.

3 _____

Turn around and around
Change the last letter.

2 _____

"After you brush your teeth, ___ out the toothpaste."
Add a letter after the first letter.

1 _____

s   i   t

Name _____

Read the clues. Then write the words.
Start at the bottom and climb to the top.

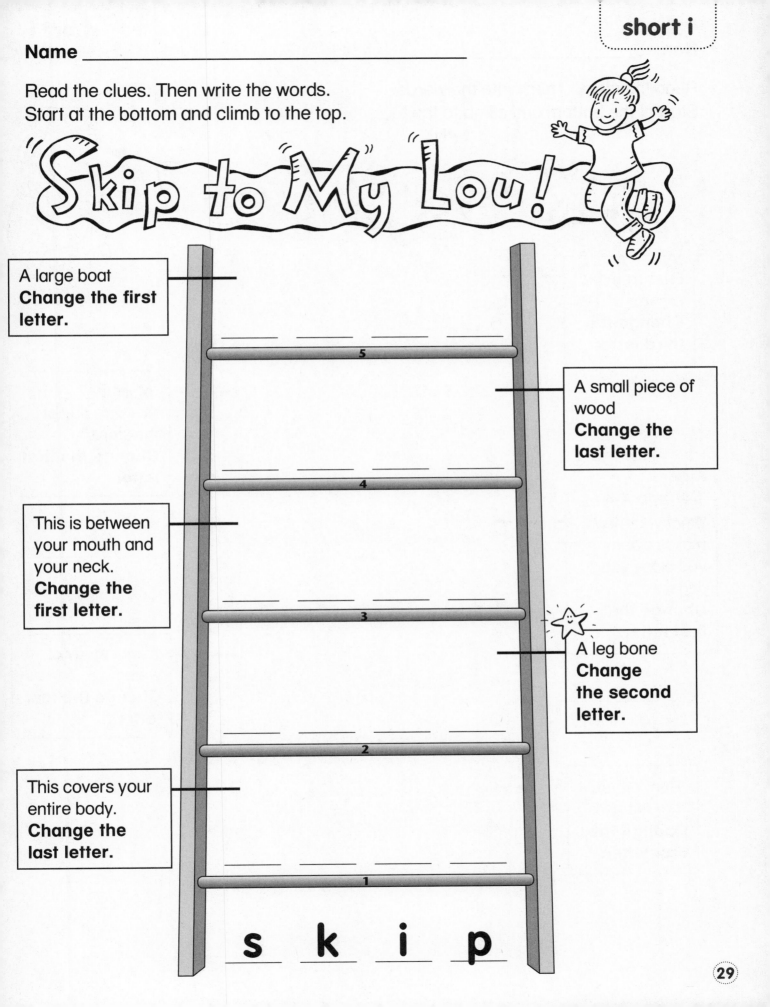

Skip to My Lou!

A large boat
Change the first letter.

5 _____

A small piece of wood
Change the last letter.

4 _____

This is between your mouth and your neck.
Change the first letter.

3 _____

A leg bone
Change the second letter.

2 _____

This covers your entire body.
Change the last letter.

1 _____

s   k   i   p

Name _____

Read the clues. Then write the words.
Start at the bottom and climb to the top.

Kiss, Kiss!

Fuzz from the dryer
Change the third letter.

5

"Make a ___ of things to buy at the store."
Change the first letter.

4

What your hand makes when you close your fingers
Change the first letter.

3

A light spray of water
Change the last letter.

2

"Run, or you'll ___ the bus!"
Change the first letter.

1

k   i   s   s

Name _____

Read the clues. Then write the words.
Start at the bottom and climb to the top.

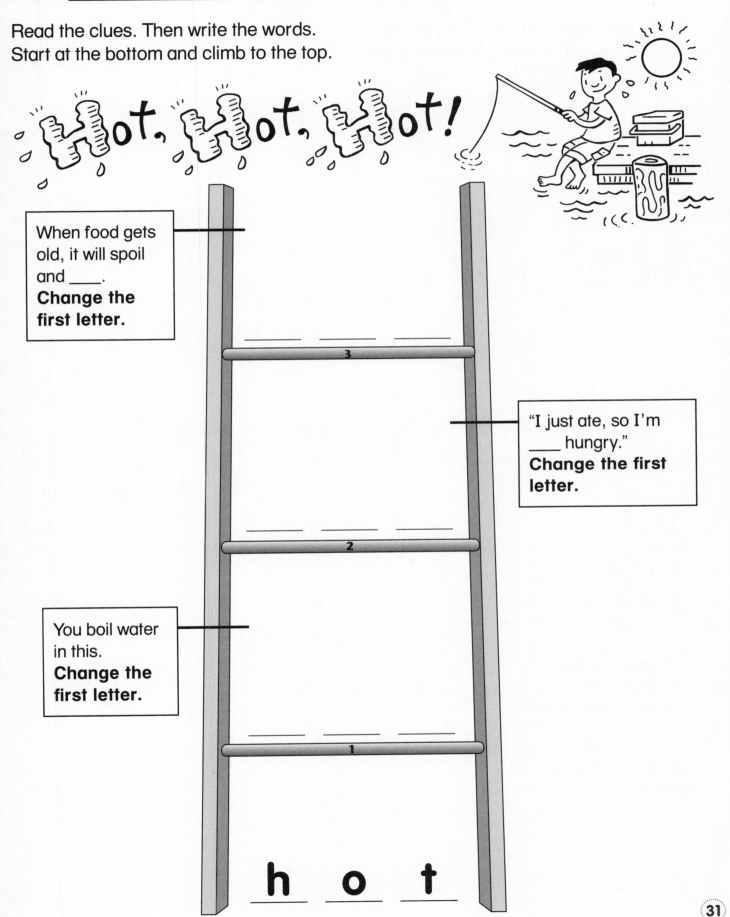

Hot, Hot, Hot!

When food gets old, it will spoil and ____.
Change the first letter.

"I just ate, so I'm ____ hungry."
Change the first letter.

You boil water in this.
Change the first letter.

3

2

1

h o t

Name _____

Read the clues. Then write the words.
Start at the bottom and climb to the top.

Sob Story

To steal something
Change the first letter.

3 _____ _____ _____

When a person goes to work, she does her ____.
Change the first letter.

2 _____ _____ _____

Corn on the ____
Change the first letter.

1 _____ _____ _____

s   o   b

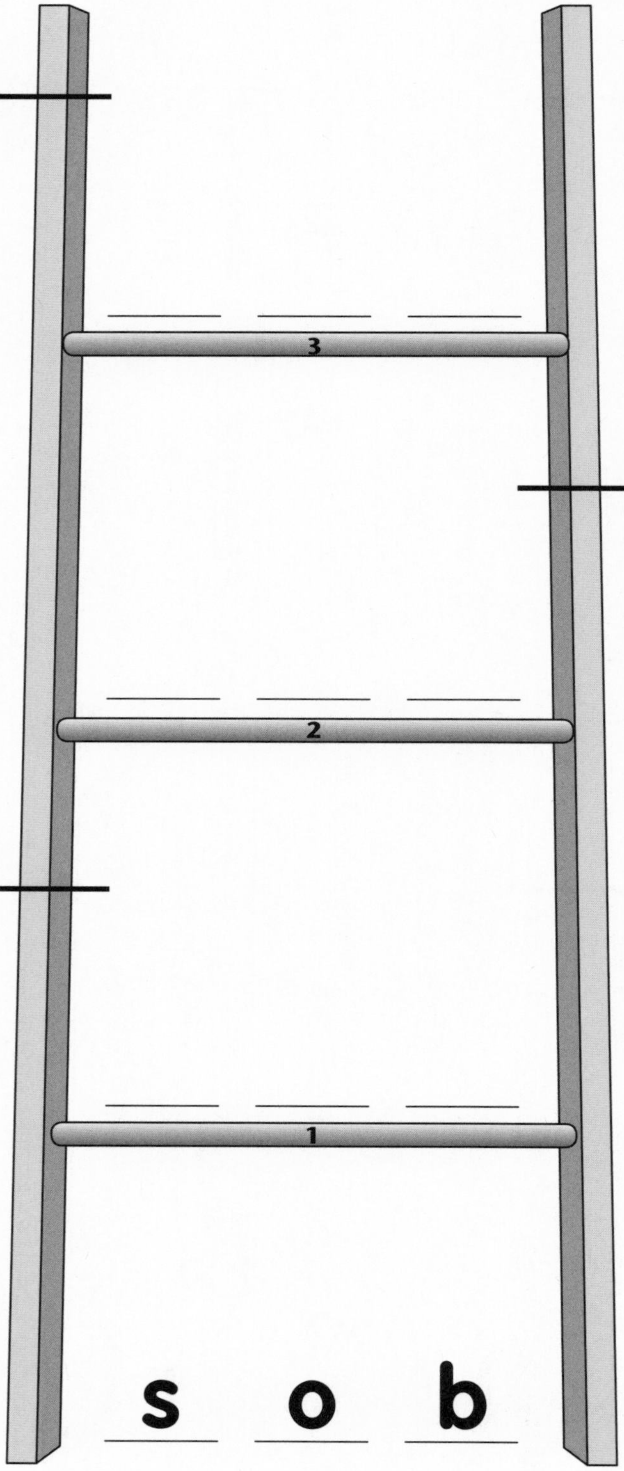

Name _____

Read the clues. Then write the words.
Start at the bottom and climb to the top.

It's a Job

A small, round mark
Change the first letter.

To write something quickly
Change the last letter.

To run slowly
Change the last letter.

3

2

1

j o b

Name _____

Read the clues. Then write the words.
Start at the bottom and climb to the top.

In the Doghouse

You cook in this.
**Change the
first letter.**

3 _____ _____ _____

Very warm
**Change the
last letter.**

2 _____ _____ _____

A type of pig
**Change the
first letter.**

1 _____ _____ _____

d   o   g

34

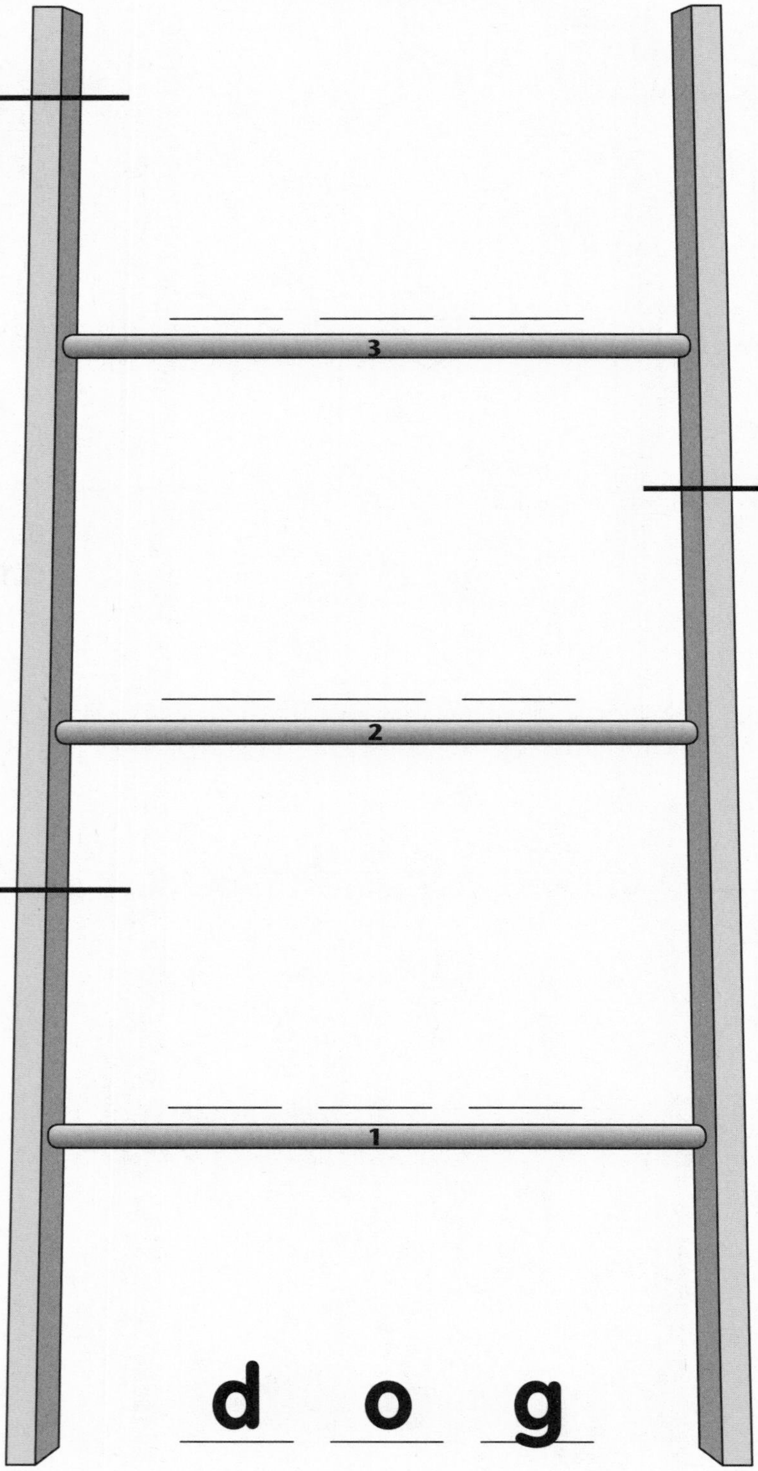

Name _____

Read the clues. Then write the words.
Start at the bottom and climb to the top.

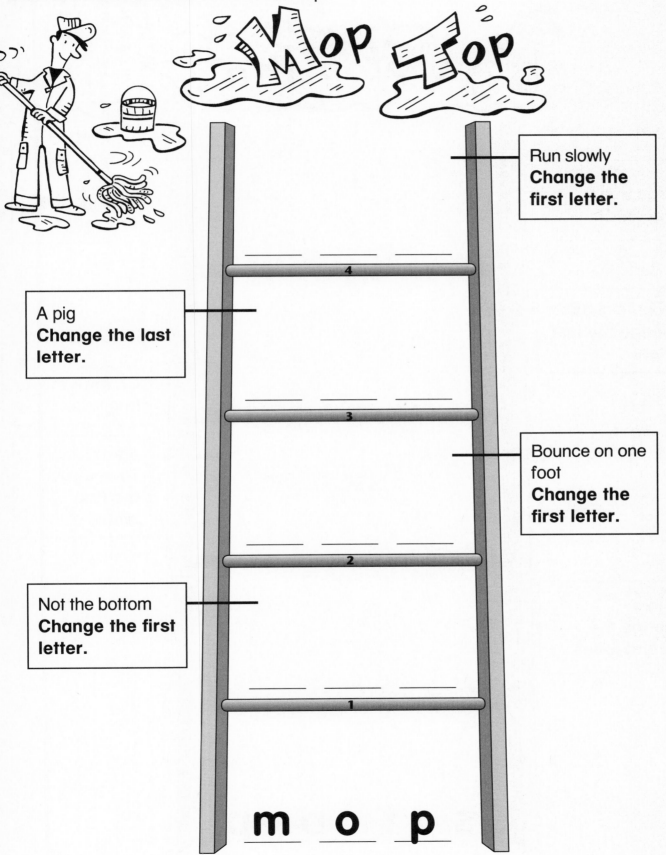

Run slowly
Change the first letter.

A pig
Change the last letter.

Bounce on one foot
Change the first letter.

Not the bottom
Change the first letter.

m   o   p

Name _____

Read the clues. Then write the words.
Start at the bottom and climb to the top.

A very small bed
Change the first letter.

Opposite of *cold*
Change the last letter.

A short jump
Take away the first letter.

A store
Change the second letter.

4

3

2

1

s t o p

36

Name _____

Read the clues. Then write the words.
Start at the bottom and climb to the top.

Chop, Chop!

You open this with a key.
Take away the last letter. Add two letters at the end.

5 _____

The opposite of *a little* is a ____.
Change the first letter.

4 _____

Very warm
Take away the first letter.

3 _____

The basketball player took a ____.
Change the last letter.

2 _____

A store
Change the first letter.

1 _____

c h o p

37

Name _____

Read the clues. Then write the words.
Start at the bottom and climb to the top.

Sock It to Me!

This tells the time.
Add a letter before the first letter.

5

You need a key to open this.
Take away the last two letters.

4

A necklace with a photo
Change the first letter.

3

A spaceship
Add two letters to the end.

2

A large stone
Change the first letter.

1

s o c k

Name _____

Read the clues. Then write the words.
Start at the bottom and climb to the top.

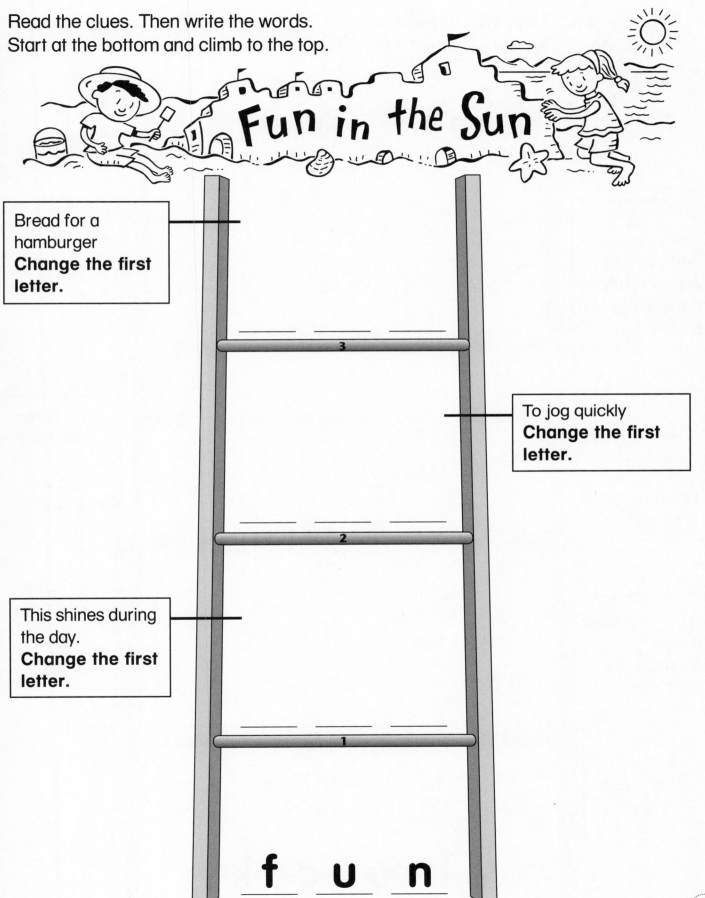

Fun in the Sun

Bread for a hamburger
Change the first letter.

To jog quickly
Change the first letter.

This shines during the day.
Change the first letter.

f u n

39

Name _____

Read the clues. Then write the words.
Start at the bottom and climb to the top.

Good Luck!

"I ___ the picture to the wall with tape."
Add a letter before the first letter.

3 _____

"Mom, can you ___ me into bed?"
Change the first letter.

2 _____

A bird that says *quack*
Change the first letter.

1 _____

l   u   c   k

Name _____

Read the clues. Then write the words.
Start at the bottom and climb to the top.

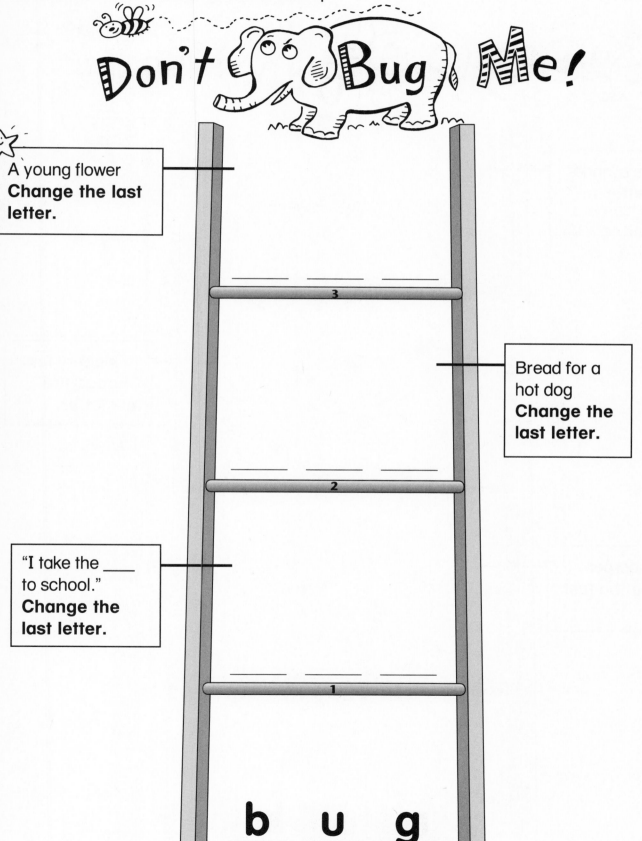

Don't Bug Me!

A young flower
Change the last letter.

Bread for a hot dog
Change the last letter.

"I take the ____ to school."
Change the last letter.

3

2

1

b   u   g

Name _____

Read the clues. Then write the words.
Start at the bottom and climb to the top.

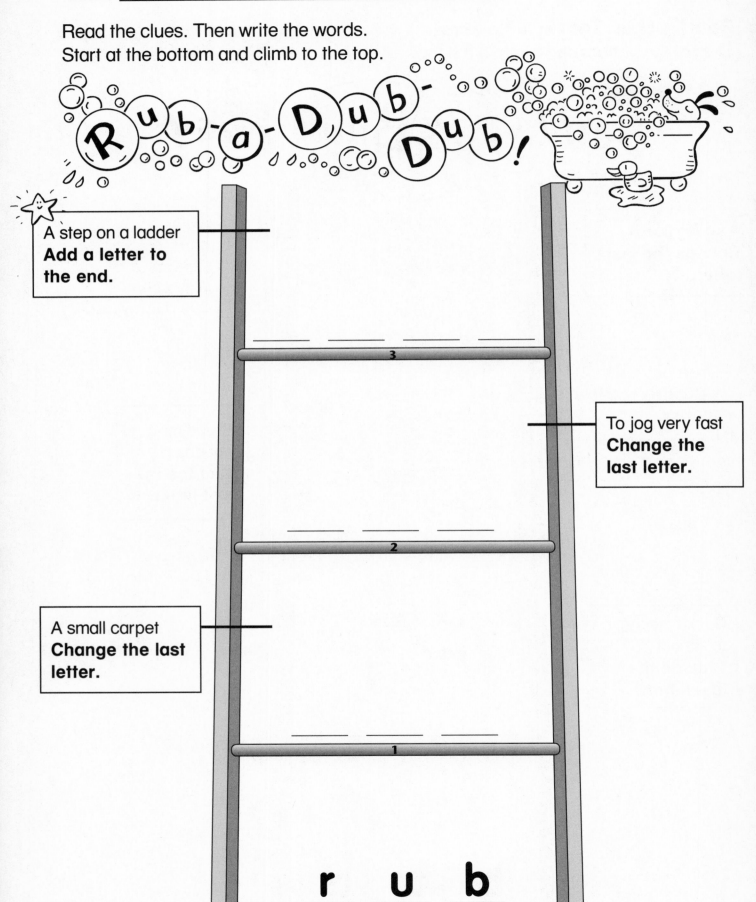

Rub-a-Dub-Dub!

A step on a ladder
Add a letter to the end.

3 _ _ _ _ _

To jog very fast
Change the last letter.

2 _ _ _ _ _

A small carpet
Change the last letter.

1 _ _ _ _ _

r   u   b
_   _   _

42

Name _____

Read the clues. Then write the words.
Start at the bottom and climb to the top.

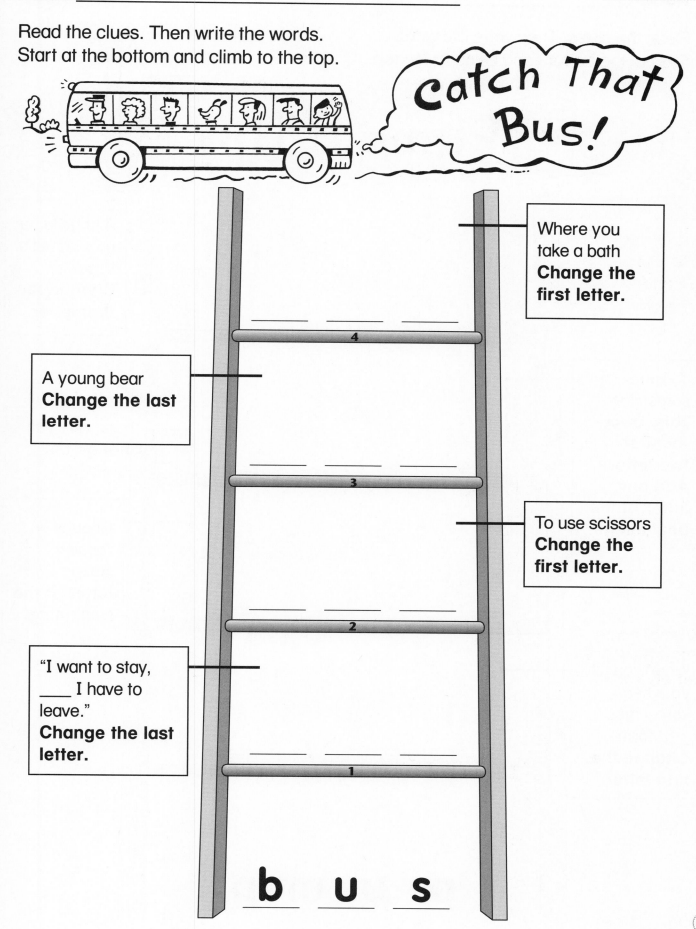

Catch That Bus!

Where you take a bath **Change the first letter.**

A young bear **Change the last letter.**

To use scissors **Change the first letter.**

"I want to stay, ____ I have to leave." **Change the last letter.**

b u s

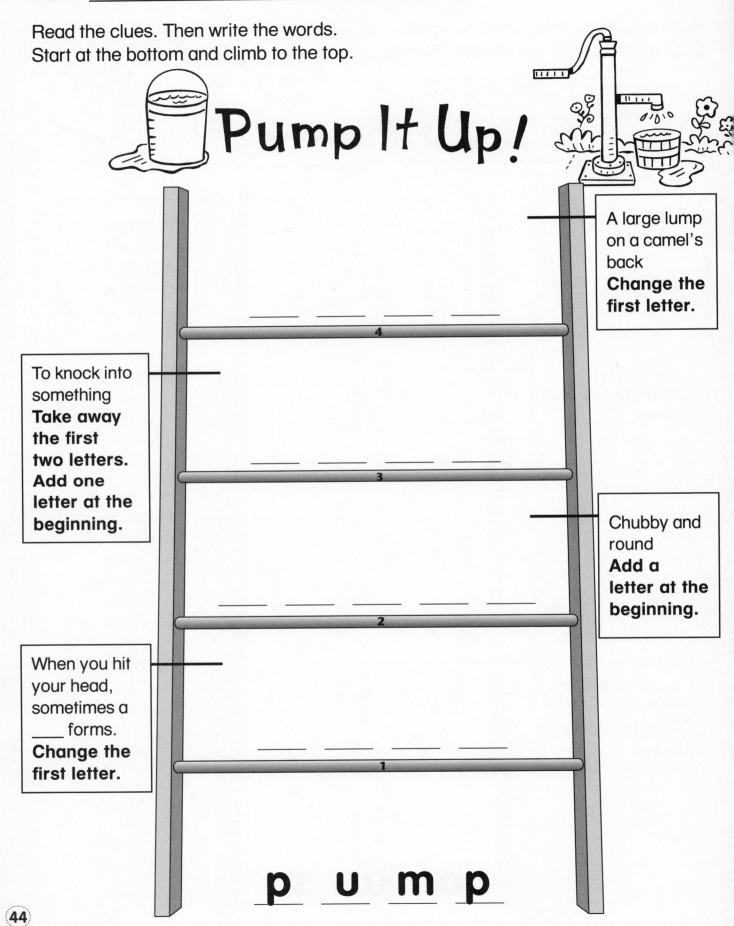

Name _____

Read the clues. Then write the words.
Start at the bottom and climb to the top.

Pump It Up!

4 _ _ _ _

A large lump on a camel's back **Change the first letter.**

To knock into something **Take away the first two letters. Add one letter at the beginning.**

3 _ _ _ _

Chubby and round **Add a letter at the beginning.**

2 _ _ _ _

When you hit your head, sometimes a ___ forms. **Change the first letter.**

1 _ _ _ _

p u m p

44

Name _____

Read the clues. Then write the words.
Start at the bottom and climb to the top.

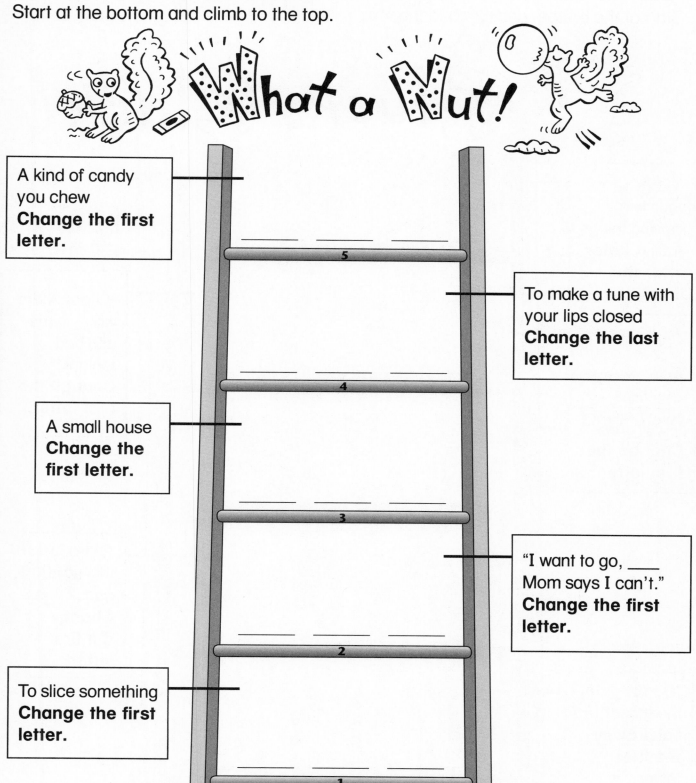

What a Nut!

A kind of candy you chew
Change the first letter.

To make a tune with your lips closed
Change the last letter.

A small house
Change the first letter.

"I want to go, ____ Mom says I can't."
Change the first letter.

To slice something
Change the first letter.

5

4

3

2

1

n   u   t

Name _____

Read the clues. Then write the words.
Start at the bottom and climb to the top.

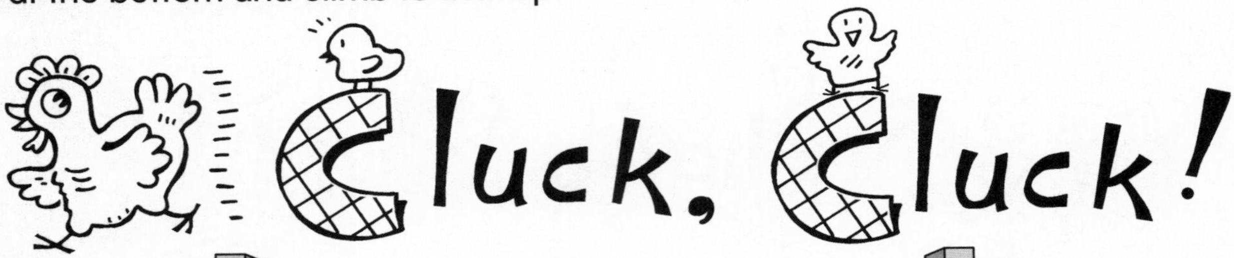

Cluck, Cluck!

A large vehicle for moving things **Add a letter after the first letter.**

5 _____

"I hope Mom will ___ me into bed tonight." **Change the first letter.**

4 _____

"Eww, gross!" **Change the first letter.**

3 _____

A bird that says *quack* **Change the first letter.**

2 _____

"Good ___ in the game!" **Take away the first letter.**

1 _____

c l u c k
_ _ _ _ _

46

Name _____

Read the clues. Then write the words.
Start at the bottom and climb to the top.

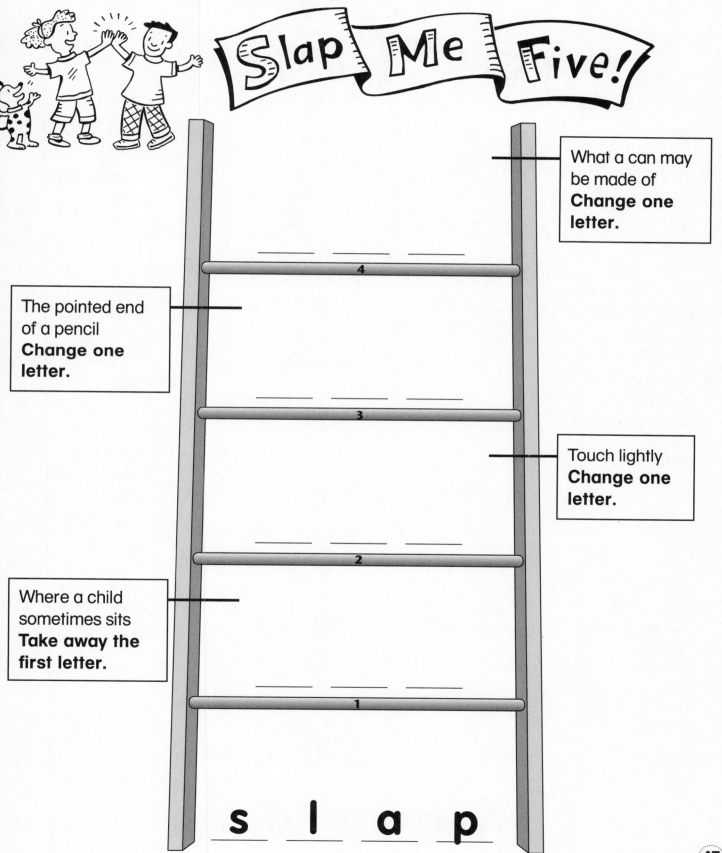

What a can may be made of **Change one letter.**

The pointed end of a pencil **Change one letter.**

Touch lightly **Change one letter.**

Where a child sometimes sits **Take away the first letter.**

s l a p

Name _____

Read the clues. Then write the words.
Start at the bottom and climb to the top.

Make Your Bed!

Mail something
Change one letter.

There's a lot of this on the beach. **Add one letter.**

Not happy
Change one letter.

Not good
Change one letter.

4

3

2

1

b e d

Name _____

Read the clues. Then write the words.
Start at the bottom and climb to the top.

Number-One Dad!

An animal that flies at night
Change one letter.

Not good
Change one letter.

__ __ __
5

__ __ __
4

"We ____ pizza for lunch."
Change one letter.

The dog ____ under the bed because it was afraid.
Change one letter.

__ __ __
3

"After school, I ____ my homework."
Change the middle letter.

__ __ __
2

__ __ __
1

d a d

Name _____

Read the clues. Then write the words.
Start at the bottom and climb to the top.

Get a Leg Up!

An animal you
live with
**Change one
letter.**

5 _____

"Put the ___ on
the stove."
**Change one
letter.**

4 _____

What you find in
the middle of a
peach
**Change the last
letter.**

3 _____

An animal that
says *oink*
**Change one
letter.**

2 _____

Where you hang
your backpack
**Change one
letter.**

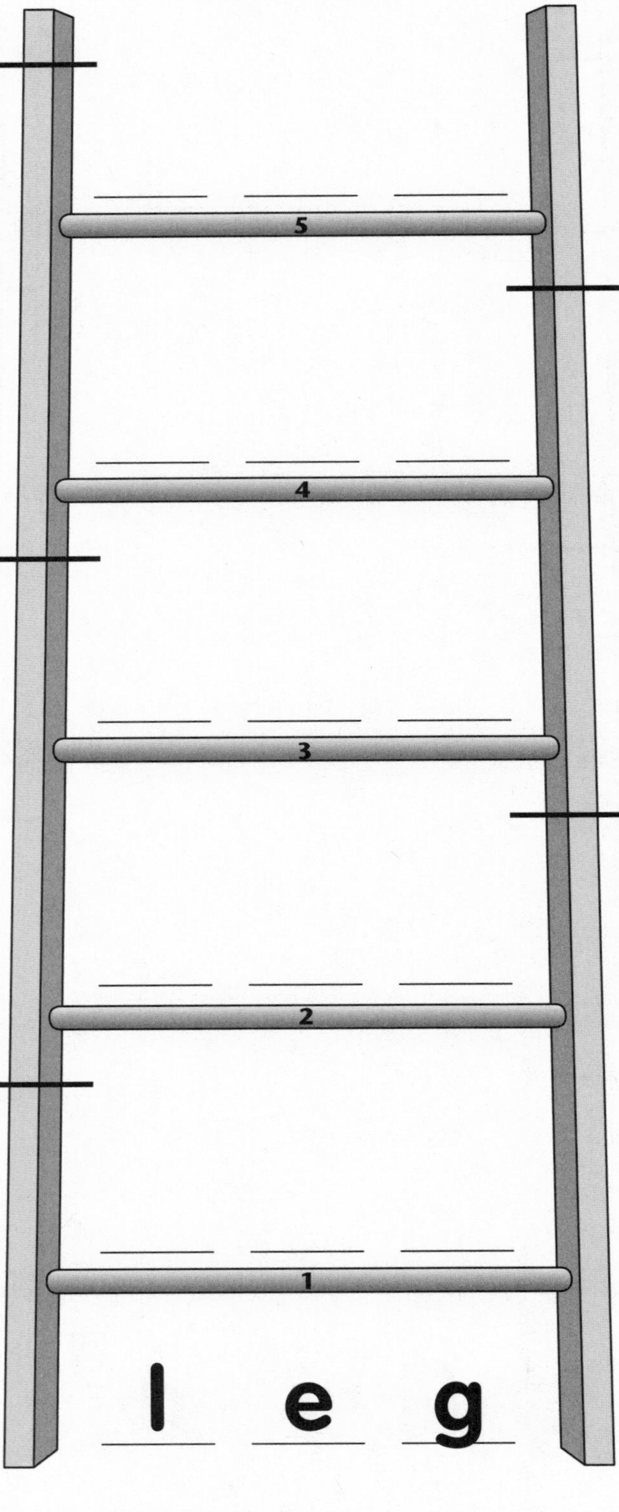

1 _____

l   e   g

Name _____

Read the clues. Then write the words.
Start at the bottom and climb to the top.

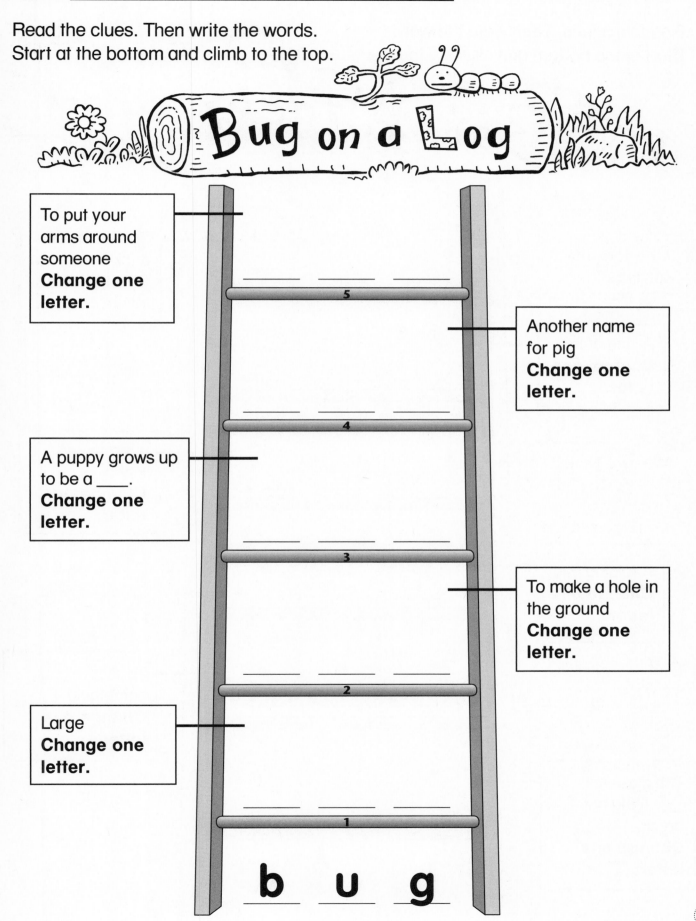

Bug on a Log

To put your arms around someone
Change one letter.

Another name for pig
Change one letter.

A puppy grows up to be a ___.
Change one letter.

To make a hole in the ground
Change one letter.

Large
Change one letter.

5

4

3

2

1

b u g

51

Name _____

Read the clues. Then write the words.
Start at the bottom and climb to the top.

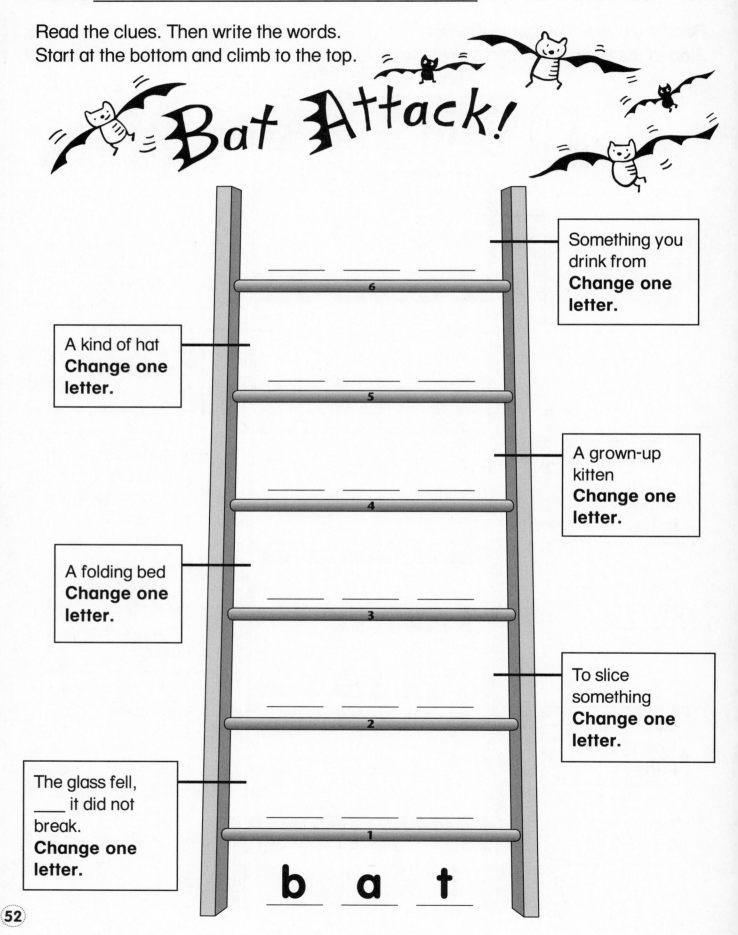

Bat Attack!

Something you drink from
Change one letter.

A kind of hat
Change one letter.

A grown-up kitten
Change one letter.

A folding bed
Change one letter.

To slice something
Change one letter.

The glass fell, ___ it did not break.
Change one letter.

6

5

4

3

2

1

b a t

Name _____

Read the clues. Then write the words.
Start at the bottom and climb to the top.

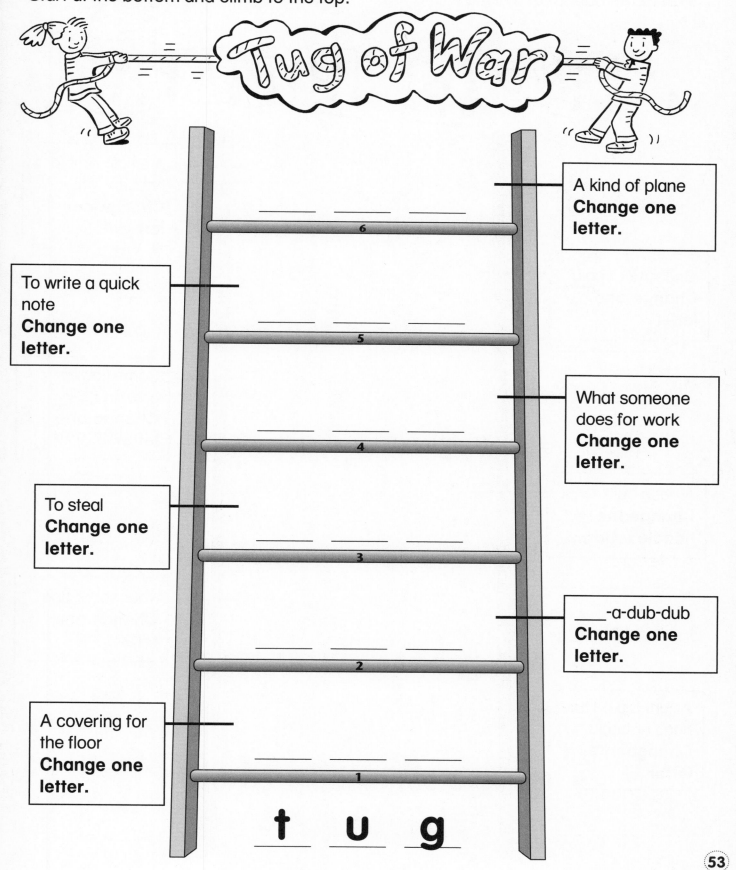

Tug of War

A kind of plane
Change one letter.

To write a quick note
Change one letter.

What someone does for work
Change one letter.

To steal
Change one letter.

____-a-dub-dub
Change one letter.

A covering for the floor
Change one letter.

6

5

4

3

2

1

t u g

53

Name _____

Read the clues. Then write the words.
Start at the bottom and climb to the top.

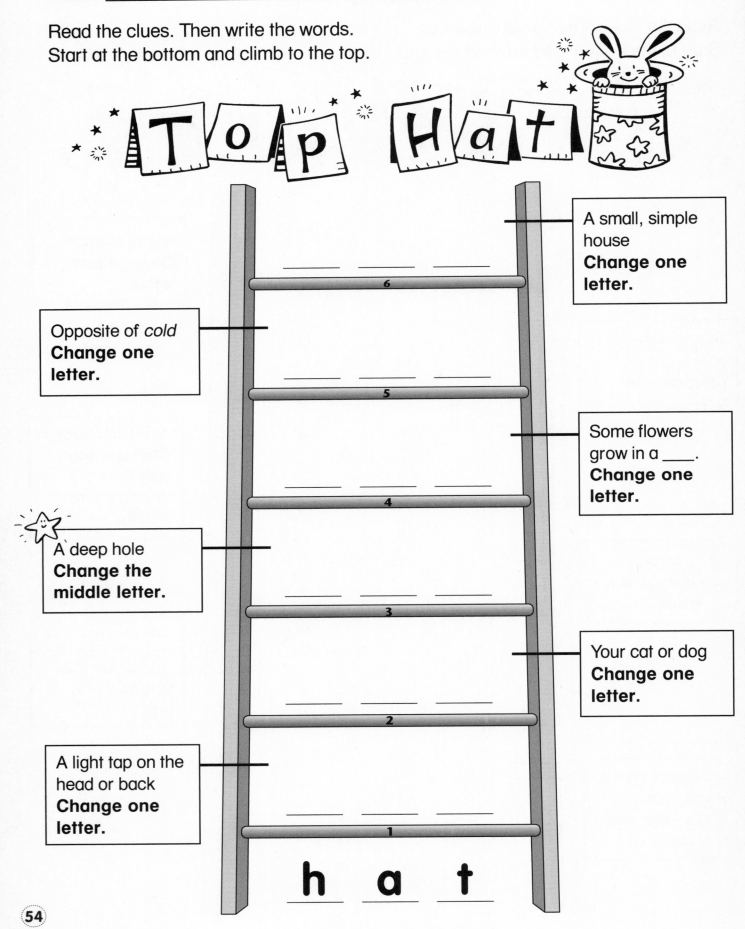

A small, simple house
Change one letter.

Opposite of *cold*
Change one letter.

Some flowers grow in a ____.
Change one letter.

A deep hole
Change the middle letter.

Your cat or dog
Change one letter.

A light tap on the head or back
Change one letter.

6

5

4

3

2

1

h a t

Name _____

Read the clues. Then write the words.
Start at the bottom and climb to the top.

Batter Up!

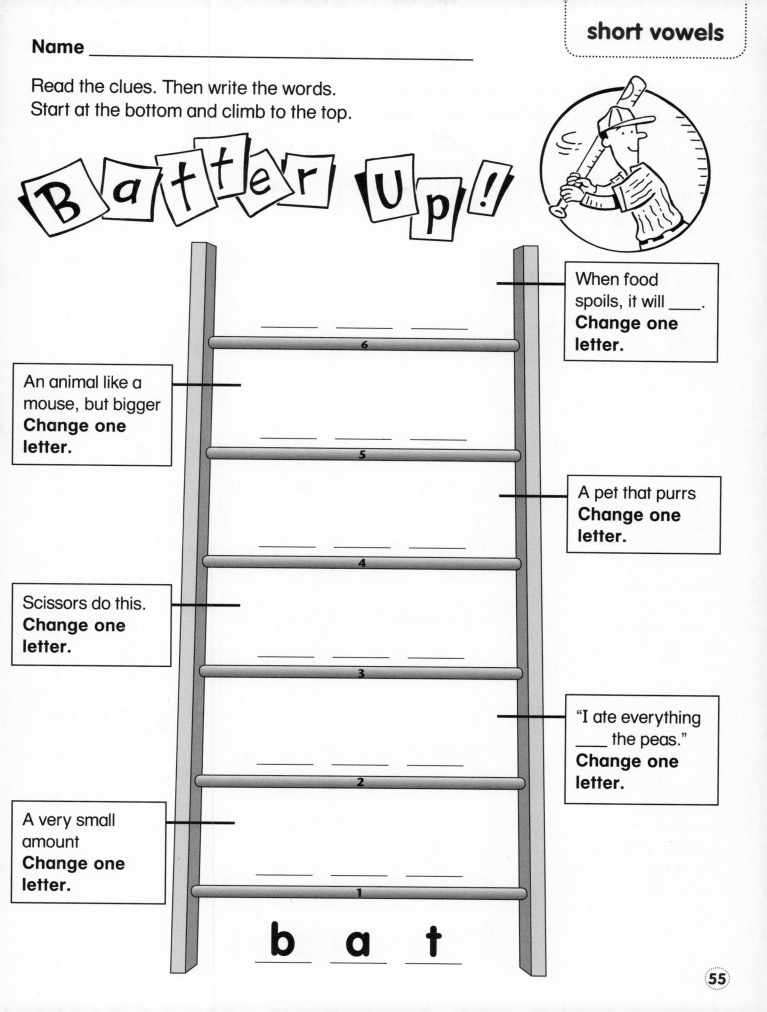

When food spoils, it will ____.
Change one letter.

An animal like a mouse, but bigger
Change one letter.

A pet that purrs
Change one letter.

Scissors do this.
Change one letter.

"I ate everything ____ the peas."
Change one letter.

A very small amount
Change one letter.

6

5

4

3

2

1

b   a   t

55

Name ______________________________

short vowels,
vowel + consonant + e
(VCE)

Read the clues. Then write the words.
Start at the bottom and climb to the top.

Tap Dance

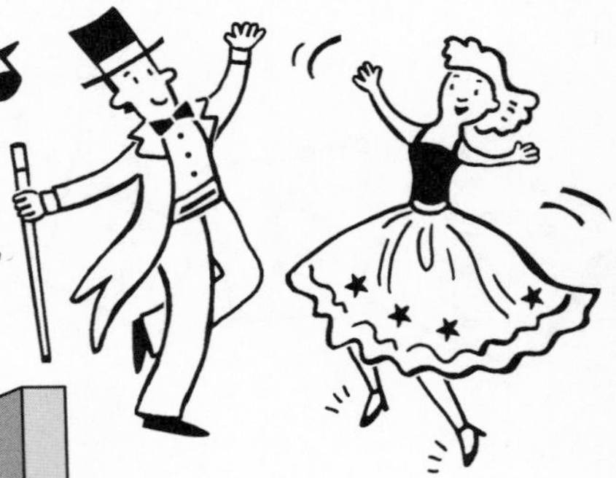

A boy grows to become a ____.
Take away one letter.

___ ___ ___

5

The hair on a horse's neck
Change one letter.

___ ___ ___ ___

4

This helps you walk when your leg is hurt.
Change one letter.

___ ___ ___ ___

3

Something a superhero might wear
Change one letter.

___ ___ ___ ___

2

You use this to stick something together.
Add a letter to the end.

___ ___ ___ ___

1

t a p

Name _____

Read the clues. Then write the words.
Start at the bottom and climb to the top.

Top Dog

Use this to clean the floor **Take away the last letter.**

To act sad and gloomy **Change one letter.**

A thick string **Change one letter.**

To wish for something **Add a letter to the end.**

To jump like a bunny **Change one letter.**

5

4

3

2

1

t   o   p

57

Name _____

Read the clues. Then write the words.
Start at the bottom and climb to the top.

Cup of Tea

A kind of donkey
**Change one
letter.**

5 _____

A small furry
animal that lives
underground
**Change one
letter.**

4 _____

To act sad and
gloomy
**Add a letter to
the end.**

3 _____

You use this to
clean the floor.
**Change one
letter.**

2 _____

A police officer
**Change one
letter.**

1 _____

c u p

Name _____

Read the clues. Then write the words.
Start at the bottom and climb to the top.

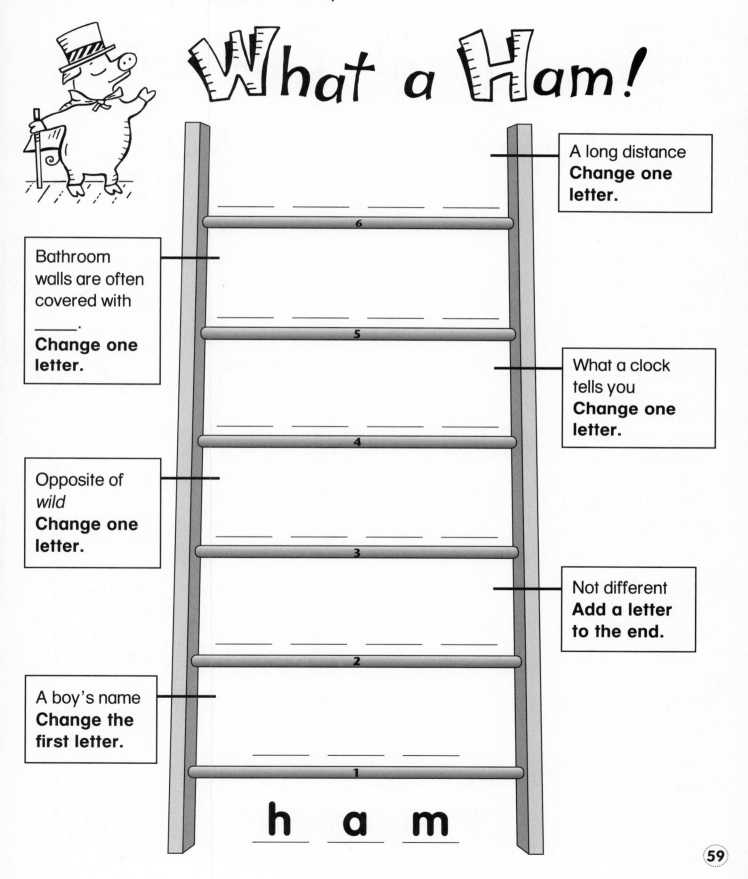

What a Ham!

A long distance
Change one letter.

Bathroom walls are often covered with ____.
Change one letter.

What a clock tells you
Change one letter.

Opposite of *wild*
Change one letter.

Not different
Add a letter to the end.

A boy's name
Change the first letter.

6

5

4

3

2

1

h a m

Name _____

Read the clues. Then write the words.
Start at the bottom and climb to the top.

High Tide

Adorable
Change one letter.

6

Turn off the sound
Change the third letter.

5

A kind of donkey
Change one letter.

4

A law
Change one letter.

3

Opposite of *polite*
Change one letter.

2

"We went for a ____ in the new car."
Change one letter.

1

t i d e

Name _____

Read the clues. Then write the words.
Start at the bottom and climb to the top.

Give a Dog a **Bone**

Opposite of *early*
Change one letter.

A small body
of water
**Change one
letter.**

To create
**Change
one letter.**

Hair on a
horse's neck
**Change one
letter.**

Something to
help you walk
**Change one
letter.**

Ice cream
comes in
this
**Change
one letter.**

6

5

4

3

2

1

b o n e

Name _____

Read the clues. Then write the words.
Start at the bottom and climb to the top.

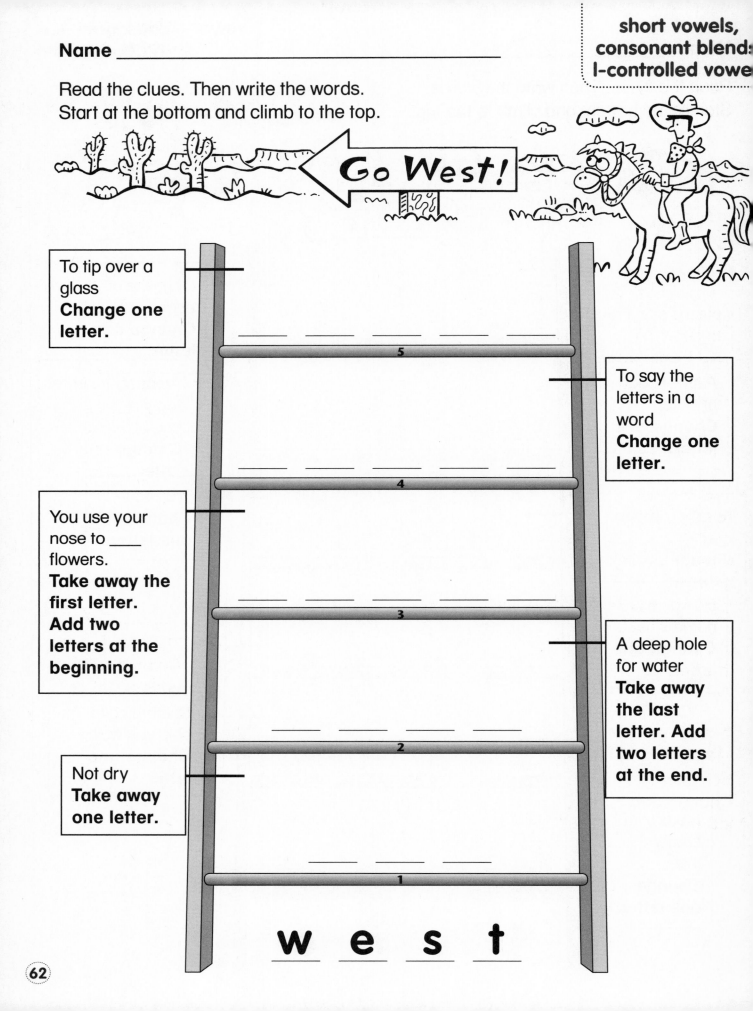

Go West!

To tip over a glass **Change one letter.**

To say the letters in a word **Change one letter.**

5

You use your nose to ____ flowers. **Take away the first letter. Add two letters at the beginning.**

4

A deep hole for water **Take away the last letter. Add two letters at the end.**

3

Not dry **Take away one letter.**

2

w e s t

1

Name _____

Read the clues. Then write the words.
Start at the bottom and climb to the top.

Swimming Along

A tool for holding two pieces of wood together
Add one letter to the end.

_____ 5

An ocean animal that has a top and bottom shell
Change one letter.

_____ 4

To shut a door loudly
Change one letter.

_____ 3

Thin
Change the second letter.

_____ 2

Non-fat milk
Change one letter.

_____ 1

s w i m

63

Name _____

Read the clues. Then write the words.
Start at the bottom and climb to the top.

Dust Bunny

A long time ago, in the ___
Change one letter.

An annoying person
Change the first letter.

5

A quiz
Change one letter.

4

When you take a nap, you lay down and ___.
Change one letter.

3

This will happen to metal in the rain.
Change the first letter.

2

1

d u s t

Name _____

Read the clues. Then write the words.
Start at the bottom and climb to the top.

Ship Shape

Something to
cover your head
**Change one
letter.**

A small house
**Take away
one letter.**

Closed the door
**Change one
letter.**

"The doctor gave
me a ____ and it
hurt!"
**Change one
letter.**

A small store
**Change one
letter.**

5

4

3

2

1

s   h   i   p

Name _____

Read the clues. Then write the words.
Start at the bottom and climb to the top.

In a Rush!

"Thank you very ____!"
Change one letter.

Something soft and squishy
Change the second letter.

5 _____

4 _____

When you press down on a cooked potato, you ____ it.
Change one letter.

3 _____

A long, pretty ribbon worn around the waist
Change the first letter.

2 _____

Small red bumps on your skin
Change one letter.

1 _____

r u s h

Name _____

Read the clues. Then write the words.
Start at the bottom and climb to the top.

Make a List

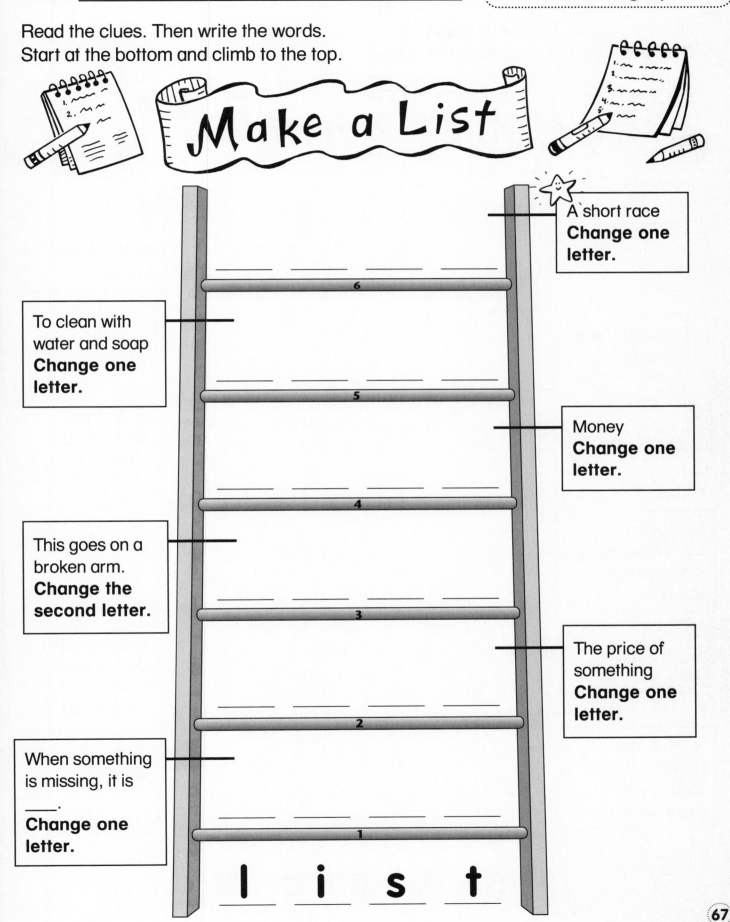

A short race
Change one letter.

To clean with water and soap
Change one letter.

Money
Change one letter.

This goes on a broken arm.
Change the second letter.

The price of something
Change one letter.

When something is missing, it is ____.
Change one letter.

l i s t

6

5

4

3

2

1

Name _____

Read the clues. Then write the words.
Start at the bottom and climb to the top.

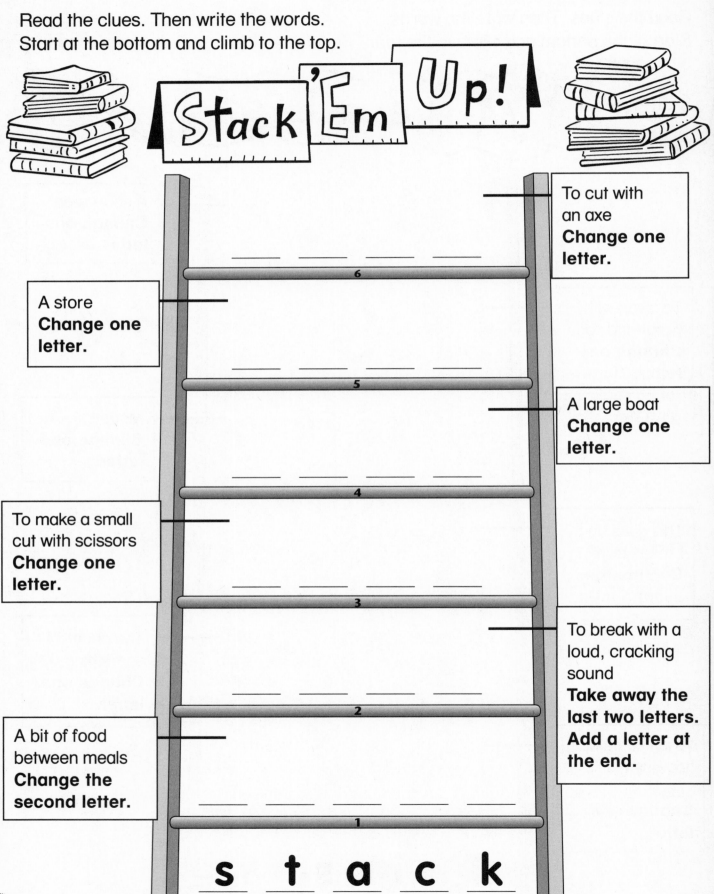

Stack 'Em Up!

To cut with an axe
Change one letter.

A store
Change one letter.

A large boat
Change one letter.

To make a small cut with scissors
Change one letter.

To break with a loud, cracking sound
Take away the last two letters. Add a letter at the end.

A bit of food between meals
Change the second letter.

6

5

4

3

2

1

s   t   a   c   k

68

Name _____

Read the clues. Then write the words.
Start at the bottom and climb to the top.

Stamp It!

This holds up the ceiling Change one letter.

6 _ _ _ _ _

To take a stroll Take away the first two letters. Add one letter to the beginning.

5 _ _ _ _ _

What you use to write on a blackboard Take away the first letter. Add two letters to the beginning.

4 _ _ _ _ _

To chat Change one letter.

3 _ _ _ _

You use this to pin something on a board. Take away the first letter.

2 _ _ _ _

To put in a pile Change the last two letters.

1 _ _ _ _ _

s   t   a   m   p

69

Name _____

Read the clues. Then write the words.
Start at the bottom and climb to the top.

Wishing Well

6 _____

"I'm taking the dog for a ____."
Change one letter.

To say something
Change one letter.

5 _____

4 _____

Not short
Take away the first two letters. Add a letter to the beginning.

Not big
Change one letter.

3 _____

To sniff something
Change one letter.

2 _____

Get larger
Add a letter before the first letter.

1 _____

w e l l

Name _____

Read the clues. Then write the words.
Start at the bottom and climb to the top.

Got Milk?

"Do not run, just ___."
Change one letter.

The sides of a room
Change one letter.

"I ___ eat later."
Change the last letter.

Opposite of *tame*
Change one letter.

Gentle, not harsh
Change the last letter.

5

4

3

2

1

m i l k

Name _____

Read the clues. Then write the words.
Start at the bottom and climb to the top.

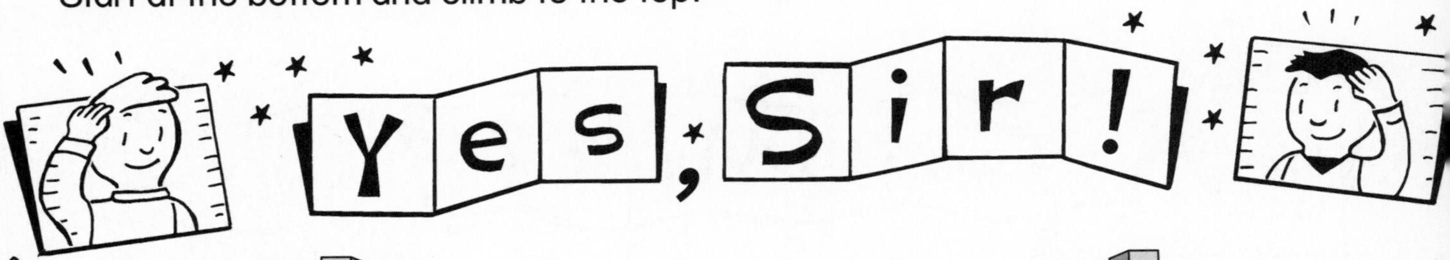

Yes, Sir!

A drawing or a painting
Take away the first two letters.

5 ____ ____ ____ ____ ____

Someone who knows a lot is ____.
Change one letter.

4 ____ ____ ____ ____ ____

To begin
Add one letter.

3 ____ ____ ____ ____

"Twinkle, twinkle, little ____"
Change one letter.

To mix something
Add a letter after the first letter.

2 ____ ____ ____

1 ____ ____ ____

s   i   r

Name _____

Read the clues. Then write the words.
Start at the bottom and climb to the top.

Party Time!

A place to shop
**Change one
letter.**

A container on
wheels used to
carry groceries
Add one letter.

_ _ _ _ _   5

_ _ _ _ _   4

Animal that says
meow
**Change one
letter.**

_ _ _   3

To tap on the
head
**Take away one
letter.**

_ _ _ _   2

Not the whole
thing
**Take away
one letter.**

_ _ _ _ _   1

p   a   r   t   y

Name _____

Read the clues. Then write the words.
Start at the bottom and climb to the top.

Sort It Out

The center of an apple.
Take away one letter.

Number of points in a game
Change one letter.

The land next to the ocean
Change the last letter.

Not tall
Change one letter.

A game like soccer or baseball
Add a letter after the first letter.

5 ___ ___ ___ ___

4 ___ ___ ___ ___

3 ___ ___ ___ ___

2 ___ ___ ___ ___

1 ___ ___ ___ ___

s   o   r   t
___ ___ ___ ___

74

Name _____

Read the clues. Then write the words.
Start at the bottom and climb to the top.

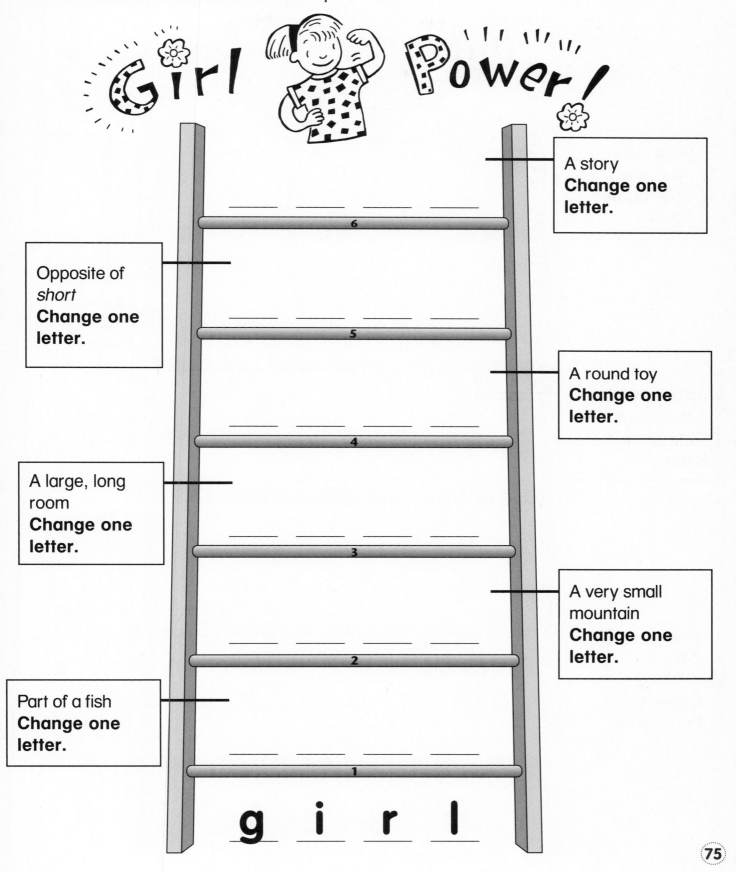

long & short vowels,
l-controlled &
r-controlled vowels

A story
Change one letter.

Opposite of *short*
Change one letter.

A round toy
Change one letter.

A large, long room
Change one letter.

A very small mountain
Change one letter.

Part of a fish
Change one letter.

6

5

4

3

2

1

g i r l

r-controlled vowels, consonant blends & digraphs

Name ______________________________

Read the clues. Then write the words.
Start at the bottom and climb to the top.

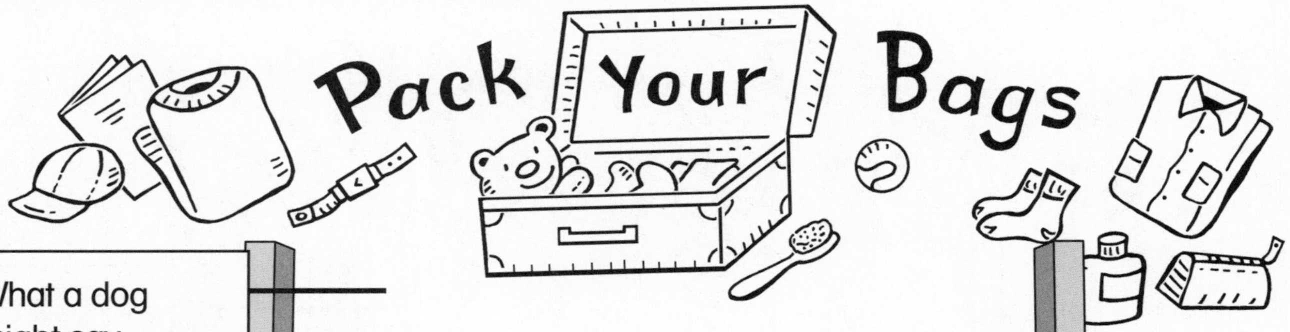

Pack Your Bags

What a dog might say
Change one letter.

___ ___ ___ ___

5

Not light
Take away two letters. Add one letter to the beginning.

___ ___ ___ ___

4

An ocean animal with sharp teeth
Change one letter.

___ ___ ___ ___ ___

3

A tiny flash of flame
Add a letter before the first letter.

___ ___ ___ ___ ___

2

A place with grass and trees
Change the third letter.

___ ___ ___ ___

1

p a c k

Name ______________________________

short vowels, r-controlled vowels, consonant blends & digraphs

Read the clues. Then write the words. Start at the bottom and climb to the top.

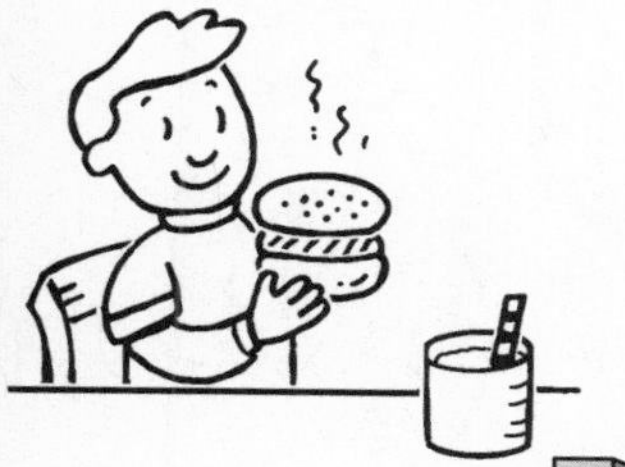

Out to Lunch

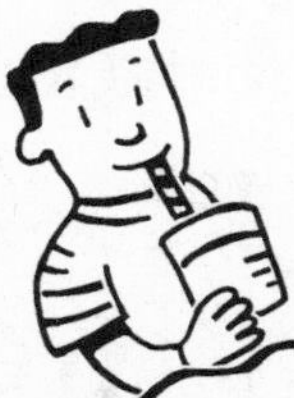

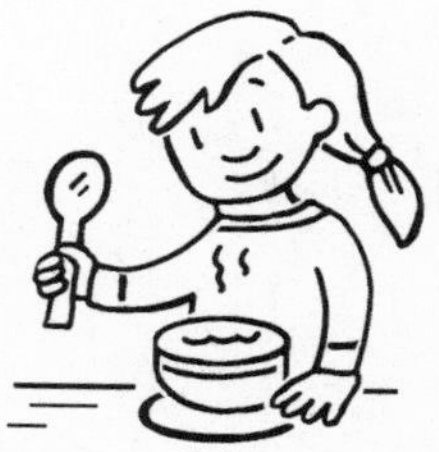

6. ___ ___ ___ ___
To flip over
Change one letter.

5. ___ ___ ___ ___
To be on fire
Add a letter before the last letter.

4. ___ ___ ___
Bread for a hamburger
Take away two letters.

3. ___ ___ ___ ___ ___
A group of things, like a ____ of grapes
Take away one letter.

2. ___ ___ ___ ___ ___ ___
A meal between breakfast and lunch
Take away one letter. Add two letters to the beginning.

1. ___ ___ ___ ___ ___
To hit with your fist
Change one letter.

l u n c h

Name _____

Read the clues. Then write the words.
Start at the bottom and climb to the top.

Looking Sharp

The shape of something **Change one letter.**

Solid, hard **Change the second letter.**

5

4

Where cows live **Change one letter.**

3

To hurt something **Change one letter.**

2

A musical instrument **Take away one letter.**

1

s h a r p

78

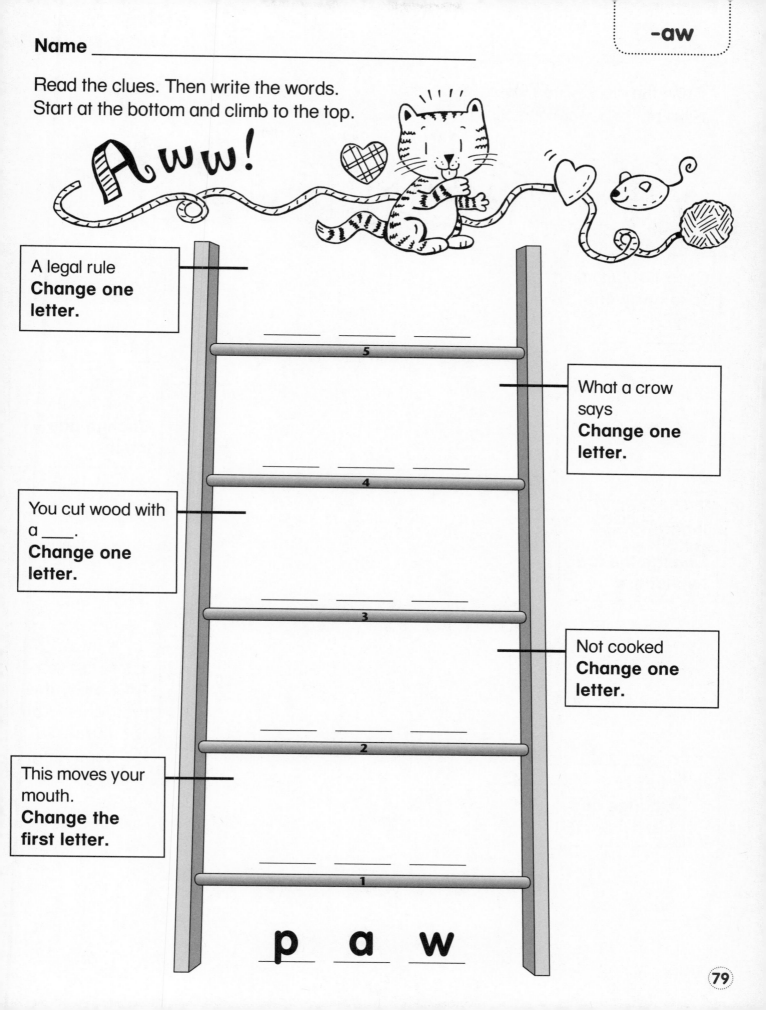

Name _____

Read the clues. Then write the words.
Start at the bottom and climb to the top.

Aww!

A legal rule
Change one letter.

What a crow says
Change one letter.

You cut wood with a ____.
Change one letter.

Not cooked
Change one letter.

This moves your mouth.
Change the first letter.

5

4

3

2

1

p a w

Name _____

Read the clues. Then write the words.
Start at the bottom and climb to the top.

Eww!

Opposite of *many*
Take away one letter.

5 _____ _____ _____

The birds ___ across the sky.
Change one letter.

4 _____ _____ _____

"I ___ bubbles outside."
Change the first two letters.

3 _____ _____ _____

"I ___ two inches last year."
Take away the first letter. Add two letters to the beginning.

2 _____ _____ _____

Not old
Change one letter.

1 _____ _____ _____

d   e   w

Name _____

Read the clues. Then write the words.
Start at the bottom and climb to the top.

Take ★ a ★ Bow!

A tool used by farmers
Take away the first letter. Add two letters to the beginning.

At the present time
Change one letter.

5

4

An animal that says *moo*
Take away one letter.

3

Another word for *food*, usually eaten by dogs
Add one letter.

2

"My cat knows ___ to get on the table."
Change one letter.

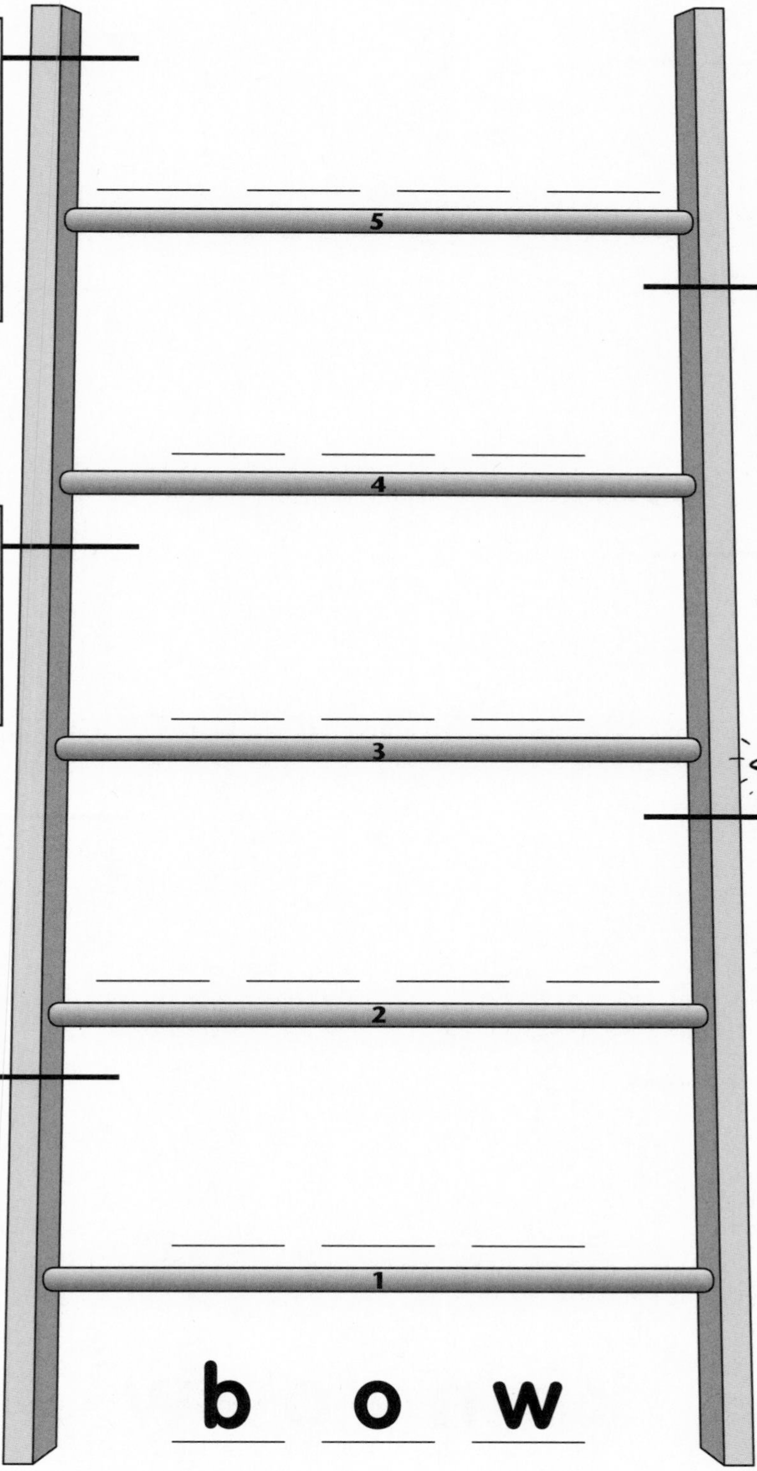

1

b   o   w

81

Name _____

Read the clues. Then write the words.
Start at the bottom and climb to the top.

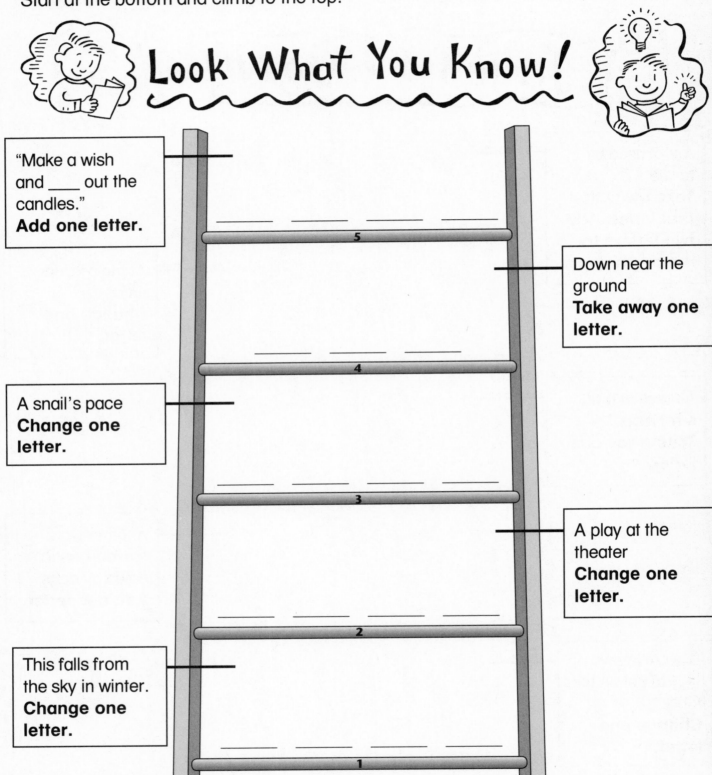

Look What You Know!

"Make a wish and ____ out the candles."
Add one letter.

Down near the ground
Take away one letter.

A snail's pace
Change one letter.

A play at the theater
Change one letter.

This falls from the sky in winter.
Change one letter.

k n o w

Name _____

Read the clues. Then write the words.
Start at the bottom and climb to the top.

Moo, Cow, Moo!

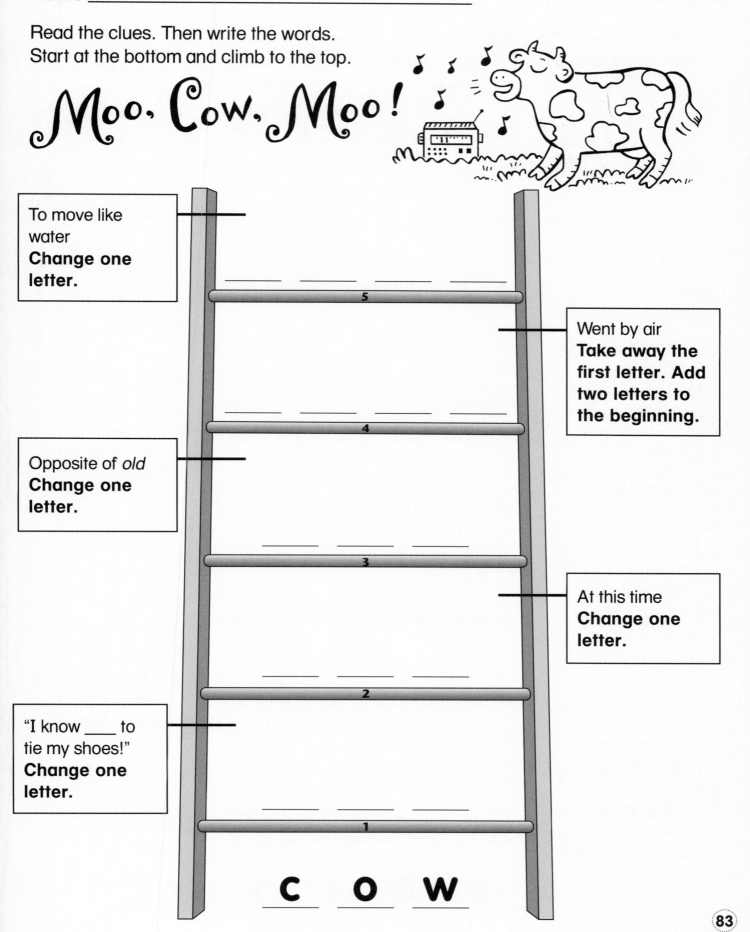

To move like water
Change one letter.

_____ _____ _____ _____ 5

Went by air
Take away the first letter. Add two letters to the beginning.

_____ _____ _____ _____ 4

Opposite of *old*
Change one letter.

_____ _____ _____ 3

At this time
Change one letter.

_____ _____ _____ 2

"I know ____ to tie my shoes!"
Change one letter.

_____ _____ _____ 1

C   O   W

Name _____

Read the clues. Then write the words.
Start at the bottom and climb to the top.

Dig in the Soil

A penny is a
___.
Change one letter.

To put two or more things together
Take away the last letter. Add two letters to the end.

6

5

Happiness
Change one letter.

4

Something to play with
Change one letter.

3

Not a girl
Take away the last two letters. Add one letter to the end.

2

Really hot water will do this.
Change one letter.

1

s o i l

Name _____

Read the clues. Then write the words.
Start at the bottom and climb to the top.

He wears a crown.
Change one letter.

The bird had a broken ___.
Take away one letter.

Something to do at the playground
Change one letter.

Bees might do this when they're mad.
Add one letter.

"I like to ___ songs."
Change one letter.

5 _____ _____ _____ _____

4 _____ _____ _____ _____

3 _____ _____ _____ _____

2 _____ _____ _____ _____

1 _____ _____ _____ _____

r   i   n   g

Name _____

Read the clues. Then write the words.
Start at the bottom and climb to the top.

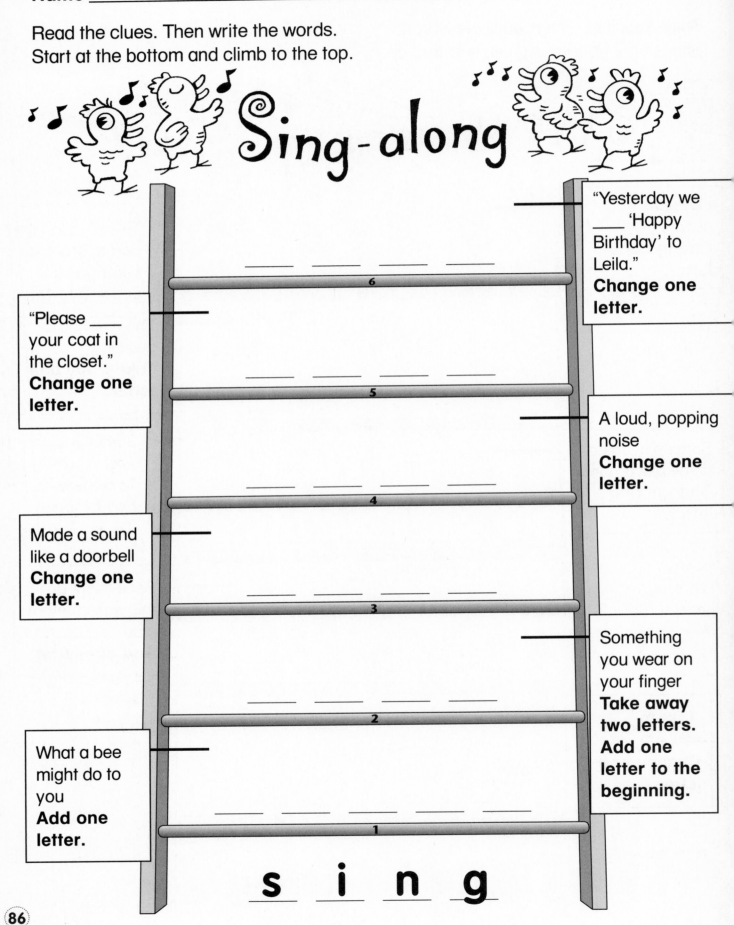

Sing-along

"Yesterday we ___ 'Happy Birthday' to Leila."
Change one letter.

6 _ _ _ _ _ _

"Please ___ your coat in the closet."
Change one letter.

5 _ _ _ _ _ _

A loud, popping noise
Change one letter.

4 _ _ _ _ _ _

Made a sound like a doorbell
Change one letter.

3 _ _ _ _ _

Something you wear on your finger
Take away two letters. Add one letter to the beginning.

2 _ _ _ _ _

What a bee might do to you
Add one letter.

1 _ _ _ _ _ _

s i n g

Name _____

Read the clues. Then write the words.
Start at the bottom and climb to the top.

Bring It On!

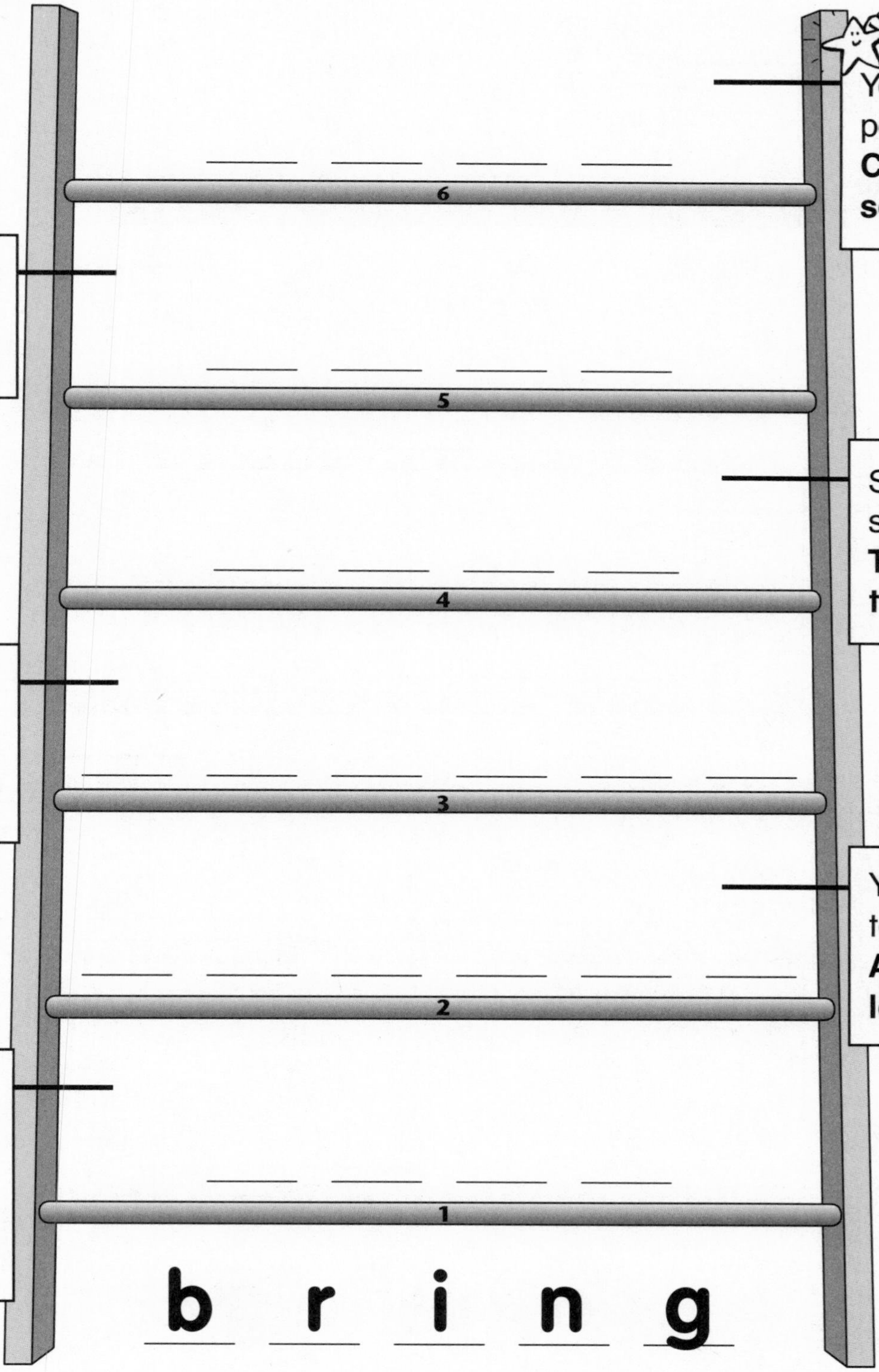

6 _____

You use this body part to breathe. **Change the second letter.**

Not short **Change one letter.**

5 _____

Something you sing **Take away two letters.**

4 _____

Opposite of *weak* **Change one letter.**

3 _____

You tie this to a kite **Add two letters.**

2 _____

"I did not hear the bell ___." **Take away one letter.**

1 _____

b r i n g

Name _____

Read the clues. Then write the words.
Start at the bottom and climb to the top.

Power Up

To cut up something into small pieces
Change one letter.

A small store
Change one letter.

__ __ __ __ __ 5

__ __ __ __ 4

"Will you ____ us how to play this game?"
Take away two letters.

__ __ __ __ __ 3

Light rain
Take away the first letter. Add two letters to the beginning.

__ __ __ __ __ 2

A tall building
Change one letter.

__ __ __ __ __ 1

p o w e r

Name ______________________________

1- and 2-syllable (-ow) words

Read the clues. Then write the words.
Start at the bottom and climb to the top.

Shadow Puppets

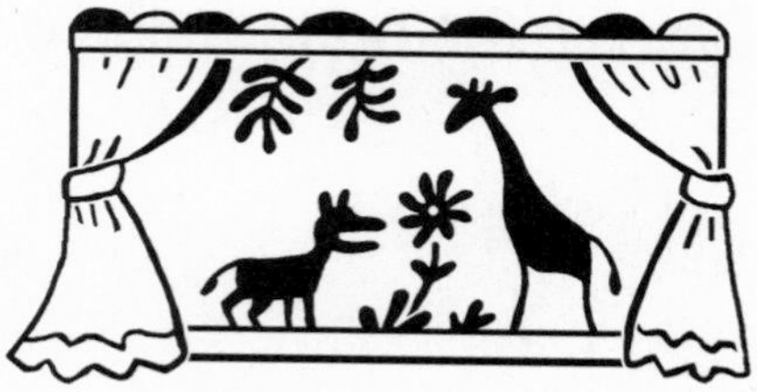

Not higher
Change one letter.

__ __ __ __ __

6

A machine for cutting grass
Take away the first two letters. Add one letter to the beginning.

__ __ __ __ __

5

A machine that moves air around
Change the first letter.

__ __ __ __ __ __

4

A tulip or rose
Change two letters.

__ __ __ __ __ __

3

Instead of a bath, you might take a ____.
Add two letters.

__ __ __ __ __ __

2

"Come see the puppet ____."
Take away two letters.

__ __ __ __

1

s h a d o w

Make Your Own Write clues for your own Word Ladder.
Draw blanks to show how many letters.
Start at the bottom and climb to the top.

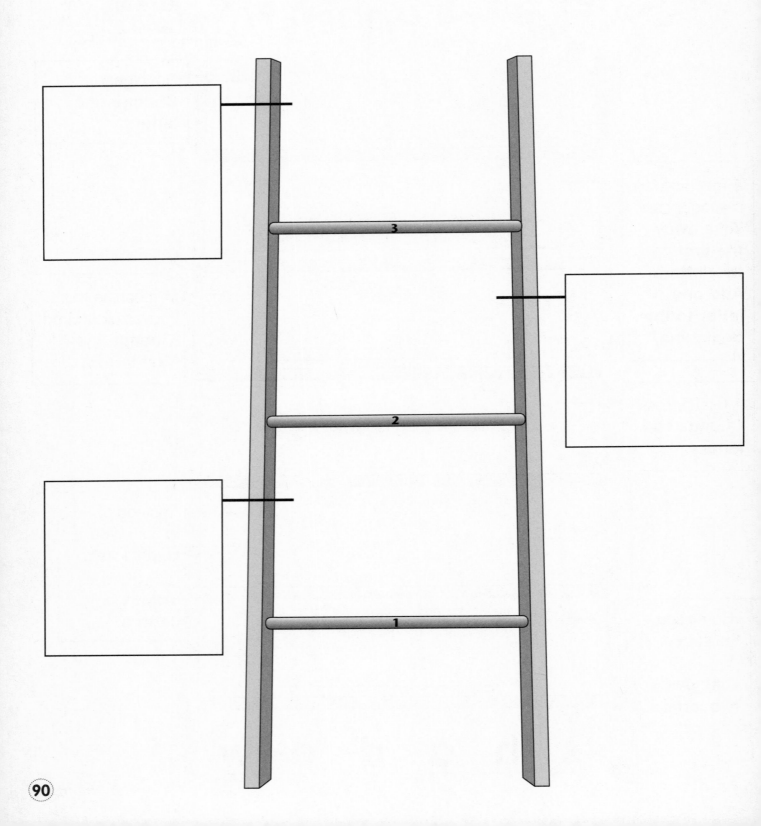

Make Your Own Write clues for your own Word Ladder.
Draw blanks to show how many letters.
Start at the bottom and climb to the top.

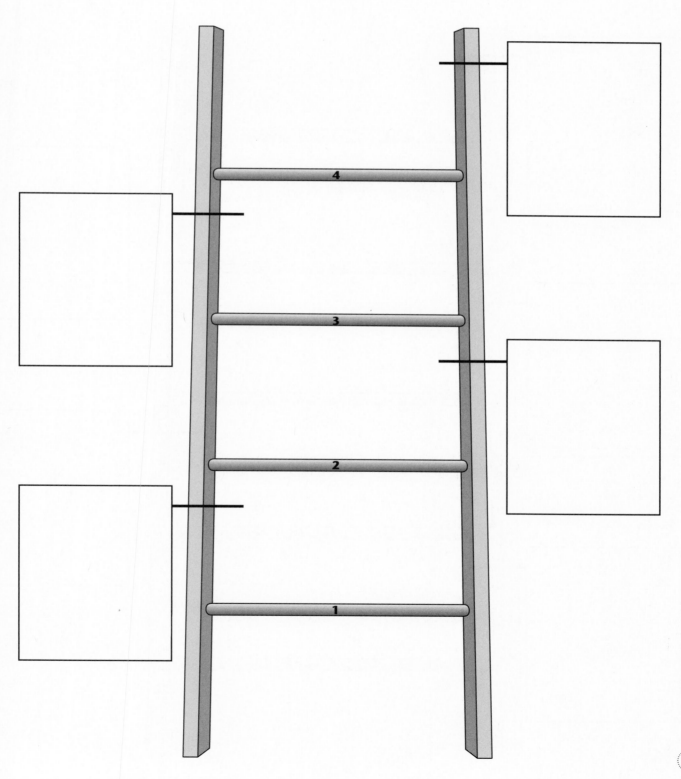

Name _____

Make Your Own Write clues for your own Word Ladder.
Draw blanks to show how many letters.
Start at the bottom and climb to the top.

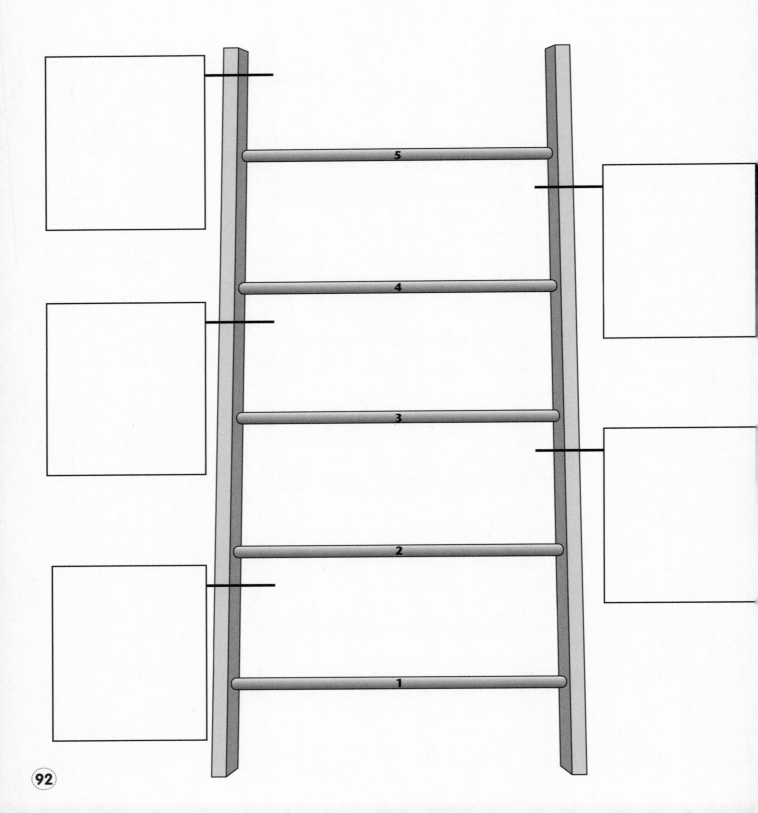

Make Your Own Write clues for your own Word Ladder.
Draw blanks to show how many letters.
Start at the bottom and climb to the top.

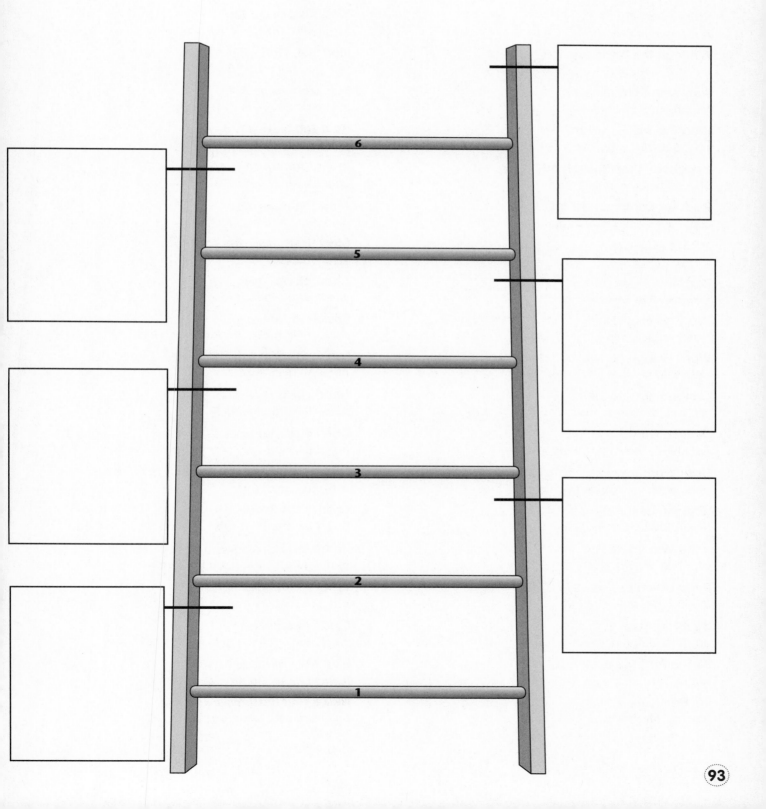

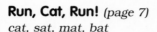

Answers

Run, Cat, Run! *(page 7)*
cat, sat, mat, bat

Pan-tastic! *(page 8)*
pan, can, fan, man

Rats! *(page 9)*
rat, rag, rap, ran

A Pat on the Back *(page 10)*
pat, pal, pan, pad

Jam With Sam *(page 11)*
jam, ham, Sam, sad, sat

Wag the Tail *(page 12)*
wag, bag, tag, nag, nap

Everybody Clap Your Hands! *(page 13)*
clap, lap, tap, cap, cab, can

Pack for Camp *(page 14)*
camp, cap, cat, rat, mat, math

Jet Set *(page 15)*
jet, wet, let, get

Bed Time *(page 16)*
bed, red, led, wed

Pen Pals *(page 17)*
pen, pet, peg, pep

Word Web *(page 18)*
web, wet, net, pet

On the Set *(page 19)*
set, wet, met, men, den

Make a Dent *(page 20)*
dent, went, west, test, tent

Desk Work *(page 21)*
desk, deck, neck, net, bet, bent

Ring the Bell! *(page 22)*
bell, tell, sell, fell, felt, melt

A Big Win *(page 23)*
win, pin, fin, tin

Put a Lid on It! *(page 24)*
lid, hid, rid, did

It's a Hit! *(page 25)*
hit, hip, him, hid

It's the Pits! *(page 26)*
pit, pig, pin, fin

Pig Pen *(page 27)*
pig, big, bit, bin, win

Sit Down! *(page 28)*
sit, spit, spin, shin, ship

Skip to My Lou! *(page 29)*
skip, skin, shin, chin, chip, ship

Kiss, Kiss! *(page 30)*
kiss, miss, mist, fist, list, lint

Hot, Hot, Hot! *(page 31)*
hot, pot, not, rot

Sob Story *(page 32)*
sob, cob, job, rob

It's a Job *(page 33)*
job, jog, jot, dot

In the Doghouse *(page 34)*
dog, hog, hot, pot

Mop Top *(page 35)*
mop, top, hop, hog, jog

Stop That! *(page 36)*
stop, shop, hop, hot, cot

Chop, Chop! *(page 37)*
chop, shop, shot, hot, lot, lock

Sock It to Me! *(page 38)*
sock, rock, rocket, locket, lock, clock

Fun in the Sun *(page 39)*
fun, sun, run, bun

Good Luck! *(page 40)*
luck, duck, tuck, stuck

Don't Bug Me! *(page 41)*
bug, bus, bun, bud

Rub-a-Dub-Dub! *(page 42)*
rub, rug, run, rung

Catch That Bus! *(page 43)*
bus, but, cut, cub, tub

Pump It Up! *(page 44)*
pump, lump, plump, bump, hump

What a Nut! *(page 45)*
nut, cut, but, hut, hum, gum

Cluck, Cluck! *(page 46)*
cluck, luck, duck, yuck, tuck, truck

Slap Me Five! *(page 47)*
slap, lap, tap, tip, tin

Make Your Bed! *(page 48)*
bed, bad, sad, sand, send

Answers

Number-One Dad! (*page 49*)
dad, did, hid, had, bad, bat

Get a Leg Up! (*page 50*)
leg, peg, pig, pit, pot, pet

Bug on a Log (*page 51*)
bug, big, dig, dog, hog, hug

Bat Attack! (*page 52*)
bat, but, cut, cot, cat, cap, cup

Tug of War (*page 53*)
tug, rug, rub, rob, job, jot, jet

Top Hat (*page 54*)
hat, pat, pet, pit, pot, hot, hut

Batter Up! (*page 55*)
bat, bit, but, cut, cat, rat, rot

Tap Dance (*page 56*)
tap, tape, cape, cane, mane, man

Top Dog (*page 57*)
top, hop, hope, rope, mope, mop

Cup of Tea (*page 58*)
cup, cop, mop, mope, mole, mule

What a Ham! (*page 59*)
ham, Sam, same, tame, time, tile, mile

High Tide (*page 60*)
tide, ride, rude, rule, mule, mute, cute

Give a Dog a Bone (*page 61*)
bone, cone, cane, mane, make, lake, late

Go West! (*page 62*)
west, wet, well, smell, spell, spill

Swimming Along (*page 63*)
swim, skim, slim, slam, clam, clamp

Dust Bunny (*page 64*)
dust, rust, rest, test, pest, past

Ship Shape (*page 65*)
ship, shop, shot, shut, hut, hat

In a Rush! (*page 66*)
rush, rash, sash, mash, mush, much

Make a List (*page 67*)
list, lost, cost, cast, cash, wash, dash

Stack 'Em Up! (*page 68*)
stack, snack, snap, snip, ship, shop, chop

Stamp It! (*page 69*)
stamp, stack, tack, talk, chalk, walk, wall

Wishing Well (*page 70*)
well, swell, smell, small, tall, talk, walk

Got Milk? (*page 71*)
milk, mild, wild, will, wall, walk

Yes, Sir! (*page 72*)
sir, stir, star, start, smart, art

Party Time! (*page 73*)
party, part, pat, cat, cart, mart

Sort It Out (*page 74*)
sort, sport, short, shore, score, core

Girl Power! (*page 75*)
girl, gill, hill, hall, ball, tall, tale

Pack Your Bags (*page 76*)
pack, park, spark, shark, dark, bark

Out to Lunch (*page 77*)
lunch, punch, brunch, bunch, bun, burn, turn

Looking Sharp (*page 78*)
sharp, harp, harm, farm, firm, form

Aww! (*page 79*)
paw, jaw, raw, saw, caw, law

Eww! (*page 80*)
dew, new, grew, blew, flew, few

Take a Bow! (*page 81*)
bow, how, chow, cow, now, plow

Look What You Know! (*page 82*)
know, snow, show, slow, low, blow

Moo, Cow, Moo! (*page 83*)
cow, how, now, new, flew, flow

Dig in the Soil (*page 84*)
soil, boil, boy, toy, joy, join, coin

Ring! Ring! (*page 85*)
ring, sing, sting, swing, wing, king

Sing-along (*page 86*)
sing, sting, ring, rang, bang, hang, sang

Bring It On! (*page 87*)
bring, ring, string, strong, song, long, lung

Power Up (*page 88*)
power, tower, shower, show, shop, chop

Shadow Puppets (*page 89*)
shadow, show, shower, flower, blower, mower, lower

Notes

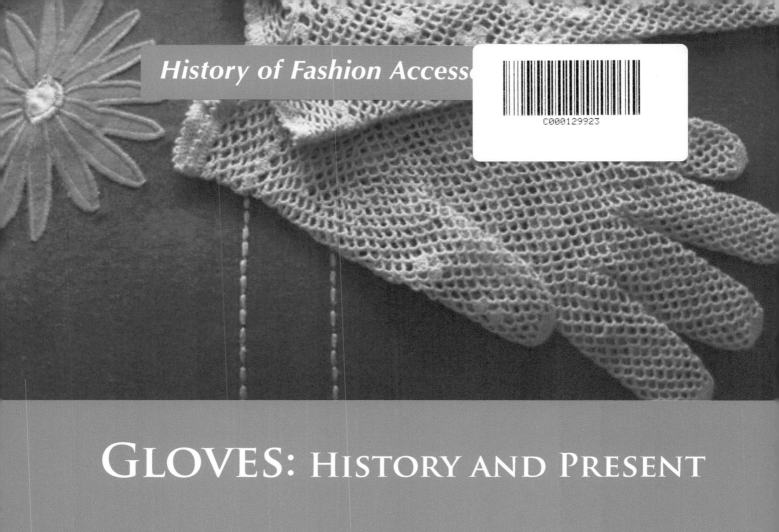

GLOVES: HISTORY AND PRESENT

Ida Tomshinsky

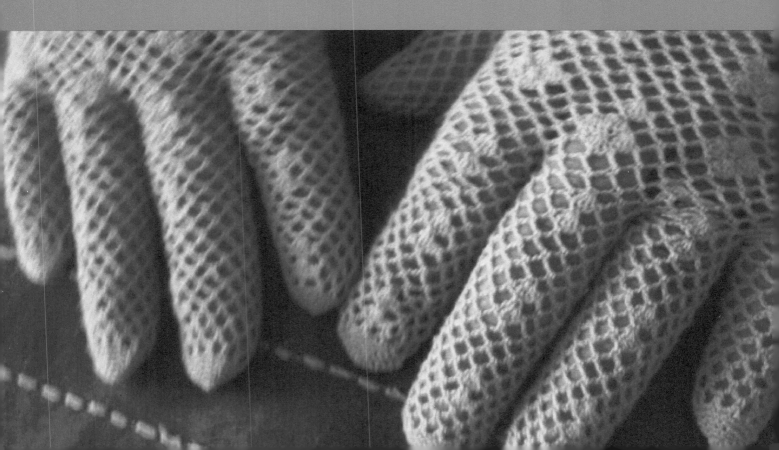

To order additional copies of this book, contact:
Xlibris Corporation
1-888-795-4274
www.Xlibris.com
Orders@Xlibris.com

GLOVES:
HISTORY AND PRESENT

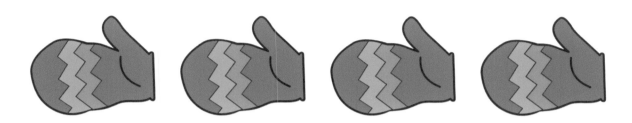

Gloves: History and Present

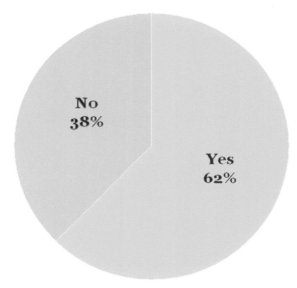

Any hand wear, gloves or mittens, protect human hands. Gloves have an old history, and glove wearing and making them intertwined with people's culture since prehistoric times. The cavemen were worn gloves to protect the hands from cold winter weather, cuts and damages in hunt and work. Currently, very few remain to cover the hands in gloves with chic and style. Fewer patterns are available for hand-made gloves. Machine sewn and hand finished gloves are mostly what you'll find in the retail market.

Beside fashion accessorizing, these days, we having gloves widely used in sports - the American football various position gloves, baseball glove or catcher's mitt, billiards glove, boxing gloves, cricket gloves, cycling gloves, goalkeeper's glove in football, fencing glove, golf glove, ice hockey mitt; driving gloves to improve the grip on the steering wheel, riding gloves; followed by the gardening gloves; latex gloves that are using professionally in surgery and forensics, and even "eating gloves" (glove use while eating - Patent 6782555.)

Fingerless gloves are protecting the palm area, and exposed fingers have a better grip and often are used by bikers, skateboarders and rollerblades. Fingerless gloves are usually made from leather. They are quite common in heavy metal and punk fashion.

According to "OMIRU Style for All" questioner's buzz at www.omiru.com 62% said "Yes" to fingerless gloves modern trend

- Omiru is a style and shopping guide dedicated to real style for real people. *"We cover figure flattery, fashion trends, and an assortment of articles aimed at making style accessible to all."*

No
38%

Yes
62%

[OMIRU asked]: Would you wear Fingerless Gloves? Survey said "Yes" to Fingerless Gloves, with a 62 to 38 split in votes.

What the new trend that followers love about these fingerless gloves, is the drama. They are long on form and a bit short on function - but keeping hands warm is not really the point of these gloves. We love pairing these edgy gloves with feminine pieces - a lacy blouse or a lady like dress that takes on a whole new sartorial meaning with the addition of these gloves. If you prefer not to mix your fashion references, you can go all out and pair them with a "moto" jacket and denim.

Fingerless gloves are useful where dexterity is required that gloves would restrict. Cigarette smokers and church organists both are using fingerless gloves. Some gloves include a gauntlet that extends partway up the arm. Sailors and fishermen wear fingerless mittens, so they can keep their hands warm while remaining dexterous and able to grip lines.

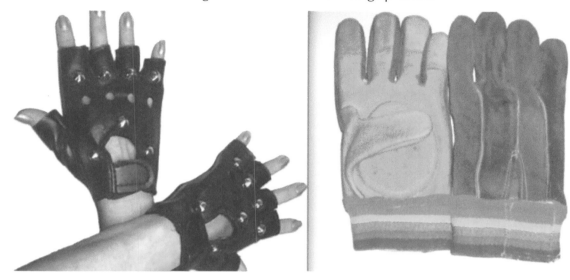

The punk movement in the late 70s sparked the trend of fingerless studded gloves worn by both men and women as strictly as a fashion item, regardless of the season.

Rainbow style gloves were also popular, commenting on the trends of the time.

A woolen pair can be fashionable and cute with a 'no' to the utilitarian, and salty. The woolen variety of fingerless gloves became popular in early 1980s, largely due to the example of English pop star, Nik Kershaw. Those leather monstrosities above remind us of the worst of Madonna's 80's fashion.

Fingerless gloves also known as "hobo gloves," due to their association with homeless people.

Adult single studded costume glove (July 6, 2010)

Gladys Geissman (Hull, Merry), an American accessory designer who created fashion Turnabouts for readers of *This Week Magazine,* is known to women everywhere as the designer who created the "finger-free" glove representing the first new glove construction in more than 300 years. She was also one of the first American designers to create the matching accessory ensemble.

Fingerless gloves, called mitts in colonial America, have five holes through which the fingers and thumb extend. As well as gloves to keep the hands warm, people could use mittens or muffs.

Mittens were also worn by working people because they left the fingers free to work.

Below is a pattern for a Latvian mitten.

Latvian-inspired mitten pattern

Requirements: size 4 double-pointed needles,

Karabella Aurora 8 (94 yards/skein) or other worsted weight yarn: 2 skeins color A, 1 skein color B, 1 skein color C; tapestry needle, waste yarn

Ladies' size small
Gauge: 26 stitches and 28 rows = 4 inches

CO 40 stitches in color A. Knit 1 row, then join yarn in the round. Knit 3 more rounds, then *K2tog, YO, rep. from * for one whole round. Knit 4 more rounds.

Switch to color B and begin pattern chart. Notice that some rows require you to increase or decrease by a stitch or two in order to fit the whole pattern repeat, and in switching from the wrist patterns to the main hand pattern you will increase by five stitches.

> ✓ **Note:** the red centers of the main pattern's boxes, as well as the white centers of the cuff pattern's diamonds, can be done in duplicate stitch if preferred. If you choose to do so, just knit the boxes entirely in white and the diamonds entirely in black.

Dark outlines on the chart indicate where to place thumb gore for left and right mittens. Inside this outline, increase as charted for length charted. At final row of thumb gore, knit row, then place thumb stitches on a length of waste yarn. In the next round, knit to thumb stitches, cable cast on 3 stitches to make up for 3 original thumbs' gore stitches, and then continue round.

Decrease for top of mitten as charted, using right-leaning (k2tog) decreases on right sides of mitten tops, and left-leaning (ssk) decreases on left sides of mitten tops. When four stitches are left on needles, break yarn, draw both colors through loops, pull through to wrong side of piece, and knot.

Pick up thumb stitches from waste yarn and pick up 11 stitches around hole left by thumb gore, continuing the stripe pattern. Join yarn and knit in the round until thumb reaches about 1/3 of the way up the thumb nail. Begin decreasing by four stitches in each round as charted. When six stitches remain on needles, break yarn, draw through loops, pull through to wrong side of thumb, and knot.

When mitten is finished, fold under and tack up picot hem. Weave in all ends and block mittens together to make sure they are the same size.

As you can see at the illustration above, mittens are gloves which cover the entire hand, but do not have separate finger openings. Mittens separate the thumb from the other four fingers.

They are mostly woolen, and many of them have different colors and designs. Historically, mittens were worn by working people because they left the fingers free for work.

The earliest mittens known to archeologists dated around 1000 AD in Latvia. Mittens continue to be part of Latvian national costume today. Wool biodegrades quickly, so it is likely that prehistorically mittens, possibly in other countries, may have existed but were not preserved. Many people around the Arctic's have used mittens, including Scandinavian and Baltic people, Native Americans, and the Vikings.

"Gloves, Mittens and Accessories Fashions in Wool: Volume 82" - Paperback (1956) by Hilde Fuchs

The Renaissance of Latvia's ethnographic mittens

I would like to bring to your attention the story that I heard from a Latvian ("Latish") person. During NATO Summit in Riga, the capital of Latvia, in November 2006, 9,000 hands were covered by 4,500 pairs of traditional hand-made Latvians mittens! The NATO Summit's Latvian

Task Force has prepared for Summit guests a surprise. The mittens were specially knitted by hundreds of women and men around the country ranging in age from thirty to eighty-six.

Each pair featured a unique design, utilizing a wide variety of traditional colors, patterns and symbols. For Latvians, mittens are much more than a way to warm their hands. Every ethnographic Latvian mitten tells a story and represents a specific region (or a county) in Latvia. There are four counties in Latvia: Vidzeme, Zemgale, Latgale and Kurzeme. I was born in Vidzeme, my mother's roots are from Zemgale, my husband is from Latgale, and my father's family comes from Kurzeme. Seeing the ethnographic mittens within one picture frame, it's like framing my heritage with these beautiful objects of tradition and culture. Some mitten designs are specially intended for weddings or other special events. There is even a rich tradition of folkloric etiquette associated with the wearing, storing and displaying the mittens.

All, mittens for men and women are different in size. Men's mittens, in general, are bigger. In addition, more dramatic and the reserved colors are characteristics for men's mittens. The colors in women's gloves are brighter and more cheerful.

The ornamentation elements are "blended in" from one neighboring region into another; therefore, the identification of a mitten to a particular region can be characterized more precisely by the composition of its colors and shades. Latgale is a land of linen; therefore linen-grey light colorings predominate in gloves of this region. Similarly, bright and joyful colors are characteristics for Latgale and also Kurzeme. Also the word "rakstaini" more precisely characterizes mittens from Kurzeme, because their ornamentation is brighter than in other regions. Calm and vibrant earthy colors are the basis of mittens from Zemgale. However, light and beige colorings are typical for Vidzeme.

For most Latvians, this project was a special source of national pride, because it combined tradition, culture and history of lasting practical value that will be enjoyed by people all around the world. Mittens are a very important part of several Latvian traditions. Probably the most popular role played by mittens was at a wedding.

Tradition says that before an unmarried girl entered into marriage, she had to fill out "a hope chest." Mittens were an important part of the chest. The most lavish chests contained several hundred pairs of hand-made mittens. They were given as gifts. Early tradition calls this giving process *dedicating* or *devoting*. The mittens were given to the mother-in-law, father-in-law, brother-in-law, and other people involved in organizing the wedding. They were dedicated to cows, sheep, and horses, and left in places where the newly-weds were going to live. The most exiting fact is that every mitten had to be knitted in a different design by using different patterns; otherwise, the maids were laughed at. This could not have been done if not for the rich and diverse Latvian ethnographical culture. Every mitten has its own story, as every knitted pattern has its own meaning and brings with it its own wish.

Most of these patterns have been derived from the Latvian tradition of idols and gods. Every idol and god had its own tasks and mission, and it was represented by one or more symbols that characterized it.

Another country with a rich tradition of women's mittens is Norway. For hundreds of years, the women of Norway have knitted mittens, but around 1850 Marit Emstad started a small revolution in knitting. During the summer she worked as a shepherd and would often carry a bolt of yarn around as she performed her tasks. After some thoughts, she decided that it would be no problem to knit with two different colored yarns instead of standard one color. As a result, many great patterns were created, and the idea of knitting with more than one color of yarn caught on. Soon other, women created their own style. Norwegian women's in the present day create women's mittens in incredible detail using a variety of needles and yarns. In fact, knitting mittens have websites that promoting mittens knitting to men. In order to make proper mittens, it required felt. The best felt comes from the Northern Short Tailed Sheep family. These animals were raised by wanderer tribes from the steppes of Mongolia and came West when Huns invaded the Slavic regions of Europe. Eventually, knowledge about felt, and where it came from, migrated up to Finland and into neighboring Scandinavian countries; and thereby, provided the necessary raw materials for them to make felt mittens.

Ancient Norwegian mitten   Modern time Norwegian mittens in two-color - wool, knitted.

There are references to the manufacture of "ladies" silk women's mittens in Needham, Massachusetts in the 200-year period, between 1700 and 1900.

There is some information about American Indian mittens before the 1800's. In the extreme climates, it was necessary to protect hands and arms against the cold. There are scant evidences that mittens and gloves were commonplace. It is likely that men and women kept their hands tucked into their clothing, perhaps covered up by arm protectors which have been mentioned in early historic documents from the northeast. In 1524, Verrazzano saw women wearing embroidered deer skin mantles, while some women also wore "rich lynx skins on their arms" (Wroth, 1970.) In 1622, Mourt (Heath, 1986) noted that only the Native American leader of a group of men had a fur arm guard: *"They had every man a deer's skin on him, and the principal of them had a wild cat's skin, or such like on the one arm,"* which may reflect the man's unique status. Some furs, especially that of wild cat (perhaps bobcat, puma or eastern mountain lion) were worn as arm guards to protect against wind and cold, while traveling or hunting. In 1634, William Wood [1865] observed that in winter Native American men wore these cat-fur arm protectors.

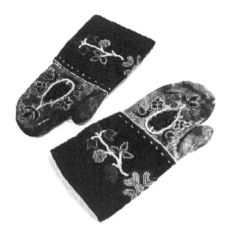

Simple chopper mittens are not too difficult to make for someone who has a little experience in sewing with leather. The most involved part is sewing the thumb-piece to the rest of the mitt. If the mittens are to be worn for work, they should afford both protection for the hands and durability, so they will last. However, lighter weight leather or deer hide can be used if your purpose is make mittens that are for special dress, and not for chopping wood. The mittens pictured to the left are Ojibwe made, from the Chandler-Pohrt Collection. These mittens are made of deerskin and wool cloth with military braid binding.

Ojibwe Chopper Mittens at Grand Rapids Public Museum & the Cranbrook Academy of Art/Museum, 1981

During the years of polar exploration many of the explorers wore mittens patterned after the mittens made by the Eskimos. They found them to enable to endure the bitter cold of the polar region. Many of these mittens were lined with fur and were very long, often times coming up to the elbow of the wearer.

✓ **Fact:** *Newborn mittens* keep the baby's hands warm and help to prevent nail scraping, too.

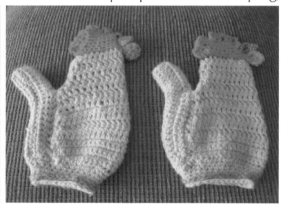

Blue and red cotton crochet mittens. Courtesy of Mr. and Mrs. Isaak Tomshinsky

In historical times, especially, in the winter time, girls wore lots of layers to keep them warm. A warm coat was worn with kid leather gloves. A muff hand warmer was worn over the gloves. So, when the girl removed her hands, her gloves would keep them warm. Just like ladies, all upper-class Victorian girls wore gloves when going out.

A muff is a fashion accessory for outdoors, usually made of a cylinder of fur or fabric with both ends open for keeping the hands warm. It was introduced to women's fashion in the 16th century and was popular with both men and women in the 17th and 18th centuries. They became very large between 1730 and 1750, and often had pockets inside. Muffs might be hung from a coat button, belt, or from the neck by a ribbon. Pairs of small wrist muffs, called *muffettes,* were worn in the 1740s.

By the early 20th century muffs were used in England only by women. It is also reported that the fashion to wear muffs largely fell out of style in the 19th century. It briefly returned in the late 1940's and 50's. In Roman times, the place of the glove was taken by long sleeves (*manicae*) reaching to the hand, and in winter special sleeves of fur were worn. In Medieval Latin there is the word *muffulae*, defined by Du Cange as *chirothecae pellitae et hibernae*. He quotes from a cartulary of the year 817, of the issuing by monks of sheepskin coverings to be used during the winter. These may have been, as the Roman certainly were, separate coverings for each hand, although the cartulary cited also distinguishes the glove for summer from the *muffulae* for winter wear. The Old French *moufle* meant a thick glove or mitten, and from this the Dutch *mof*, Walloon *mouffe*, and thence English "muff," are probably derived.

"Winter aka Woman with a Muff"
by Berthe Morisot from
Dallas Museum of Arts, 1880

First gloves were found in Egyptian pyramids. Primarily the gloves were available in the shape of bags, without finger holes and resembled the mittens. Egyptian women protected their hands during work and meals. The ancient Egyptians, Greeks and Romans all wore gloves. *The Minoan Youth Boxing,* Knossos fresco, is the earliest documented use of gloves.

Gloves are seen in ancient writings, such as Homer's "The Odyssey,"in which Laertes is said to wear gloves in his garden so as to avoid the brambles. There is some debate over the translation of this text. In "The History of Herodotus," written in 440 BC, Herodotus describes how Leotychides was given a bribe in the form of a gauntlet overflowing with silver, which later incriminated him. Among the Romans also there are occasional references to the use of gloves. According to Pliny, the the Younger (ca. 100), his uncle, shorthand writer, wore gloves during the winter so as not to impede the elder Pliny's work. Often the peasants in these societies wore three-fingered gloves, while the aristocracy wore five-fingered ones.

During the 13th century, gloves began to be worn by ladies as a fashion ornament. They were made of linen and silk, and, sometimes, reached to the elbow. They were worn not only by holy women, according guidance written in early thirteenth-century *Ancrene Wisse*. Sumptuary laws were in place to restrain this vanity against samile gloves in Bologna in 1294 and against gloves in Rome in 1560. Samile was luxurious and heavy silk fabric worn in Middle Ages that often included silver and golden threads.

A Paris corporation or guild of gantiers (glover-makers) existed from the thirteenth century. They made gloves in skin or in fur.

In England, after the Norman Conquest, royalty and dignitaries wore gloves as a badge of distinction. The glove became meaningful, and it was going both ways, as social and as a fashion statement. It became custom to fling a gauntlet at the feet of an opponent challenging integrity and inviting to satisfaction it by a duel. The glove to challenge personal battles became an integral part of English Law for nearly 800 years. It was a right that any free man could claim.

In the twelfth century, gloves became a part of the fashionable dress. Every well-dressed woman would appear in public in gloves. In fourteenth century, knights were wearing gloves under their plated gauntlets for added strength.

Pair of gloves, 1603-1625 at Victoria & Albert Museum

The effigies of the medieval kings such as King Henry II, Richard I, and King John, all show them wearing gloves decorated with jewels. King John's gloves were also embroidered. Imagine how these gloves glittered with diamonds and rubies amidst the splendor of the Court! Mary, Queen of Scots, owned beautifully made gloves embroidered with gold and silver and decorated with pearls.

Gloves became more accessible to the common people, and their popularity grew. However, it was not until the sixteenth century that they reached their greatest elaboration, when Queen Elizabeth I (1533-1603) set the fashion for wearing them richly embroidered and jeweled. As the story goes, she was putting her gloves on and taking them off during the audiences, to draw attention to her beautiful hands. The Queen Elizabeth I was so fond of gloves that she amassed more than 2,000 pairs which were looked after by a special wardrobe mistress.

It is an interesting fact that nobles gave her many of these gloves as presents. Some were New Year's gifts; it was apparently the custom of English monarchs to ask their subjects for presents for the New Year. Queen Elizabeth I also gave gloves to aristocrats as presents. For example, she gave George de Clifford, the Earl of Northumberland a pair. He had them encrusted with diamonds and must treasured them as a gift from his Queen.

In 16th and 17th centuries, gloves were made from leather, linen, silk or lace, and sometimes, fringed. After seventeenth century, emphasis was on proper fit, and gloves became less ornamental. In fact, gloves were so popular that they were given as keepsakes to wedding guests, a tradition that continued into the nineteenth century.

London had become the hub of glove trade. The craft had been protected against foreign imports. In 1826 the barrier against imports was swept away in favor of the 19th century philosophy of free trade.

In Paris, the gantiers became gantiers-perfumers, for the scented oils and musk that perfumed leather gloves. Makers of knitted gloves did not retain perfume and had less social cachet, were organized in a separate guild of bonnetiers. They made knit gloves from silk and wool. Knitted gloves were a refined handiwork that required five years of apprenticeship; defective work was subject to confiscation and burning.

Embroidered and jeweled gloves also formed part of the emblem of emperors and kings. For example, Matthew of Paris, in recording the burial of Henry II of England in 1189, mentions that he was buried in his coronation robes with a golden crown on his head and gloves on his hands. Gloves were also found on the hands of King John when his tomb was opened in 1797 and on King Edward I when his tomb was opened in 1774.

As a part of the liturgical ornaments, pontifical gloves were used primarily by the pope, the cardinals, and bishops. They may be worn only at the celebration of mass. Their introduction may have been due to a simple desire to keep the hands clean for the holy mysteries, but also they were adopted as part of the increasing pomp with which the bishops were surrounding themselves. Sir Walter Scott once said, "A glove is an emblem of the faith."

The Insignia of the Holy Roman Empire is a set of various items of clothing collected and made over a period of many years that were used by various Emperors of the empire. The robes and other items were often used only on state occasions such as coronations. The gloves below were made in the early 13th century for the coronation of Emperor Frederick II. The gloves images below were kindly provided by Prof. Michael Greenhalgh from his private collection. As with many of the other spectacular garments that make up the Insignia of Holy Roman Empire, the gloves were made in the Royal Workshops of Sicily. These gloves were worn by the Emperor at his coronation in 1220.

Gloves of Frederick II

The gloves decorations include applied pearls, emeralds, rubies, sapphires and enameled plaques. The materials include red silk and gold wired embroidery. The palms of the gloves are worked in the design of single-headed eagle, using gold thread, and underside couching.

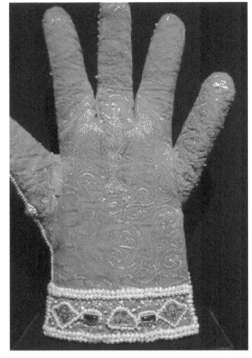

Detail of the glove   Detail of palm of the glove

The Great War brought an expanding engineering industry to the cities and altered the labor situation. There was a greater use of capital and division of labor between men who dressed the leather, and the women who sewed them. Industrial revolution brought new changes and the establishment of glove sizes and method of cutting. The French Master Glover, Xavier Jouvin (1800-1844), uniformed the glove making process in grading for size, giving a constant shape for the makers establishing a reliable fit, and at relatively cheap cost.

Ladies in early 19th century adored opera gloves. One oddity is that they tried to fit their hands into gloves a size too small! This forced the hand to rest in half cupped position, perfect for greeting, but not for kissing. Buttonhook and powdered alum provided some lubrication. Determined women would sit for hours, coaxing their hands down into tight gloves. Sometimes, a pair of opera gloves would have up to sixteen buttons and required to use glove stretchers; plus the nimble hands of a maid. Few books remain that give us a real insight of early gloves. One of the more revered in existence today is *Le Gant*. This book, while entirely in French, reveals many patterns, brief development, and history of the glove. There are passages telling us of the period's social aspects and sexual significance pertaining to the glove including insulation from the heat or cold, protection from scratches and cuts, bold or minute fashion statements.

Gloves have worn many hats, so to speak figurative, throughout history. They continue to be a wholly integrated part of many professions today.

Norma Shephard in the *Glove Story: A History of Women's Gloves* [Gouts] stated, *"by 1901, manicurists were cutting into the gloves' business, leaving commentators to lament the disappearance of beautiful gloves.* London's *"What's What"* reported *"many creations cry aloud for appropriate gloves to complete them… and fashion appears inclined to discard them altogether."* Ms. Shephard continues, *"It may have been the influenza epidemic that returned this fashion accessory to its former glory, as before the modern age of antibiotics, gloves were more than fashion staple, they were a hygienic necessity."*

The best-known type of evening glove, the "mousquetaire," got their name due to the wrist-level opening, most commonly three inches long. The mousquetaire is originally derived from the gauntlets worn by French musketeers of the 16th and 17th centuries. According to Ambrose Bierce in "The Devil's Dictionary" (1911) the definition of long glove is stated below -

✓ **Note:** "Mousquetaire, n. A long glove covering a part of the arm. Worn in New Jersey. "Mousquetaire" is a mighty poor way to spell "musketeer."

Mousquetaire gloves have buttons at the wrist, so the wearer could open the buttons and skip her hand out without taking the whole glove off. This is how ladies wore gloves while dinning. After the meal, they would put their hands back into the gloves, usually for the rest of the evening. They were most popular in the Victorian era.

In the Victorian and Edwardian periods, it was considered absolutely essential for a lady or gentleman to keep their gloves on at all times, even when bathing, and kid gloves were supposed to be skintight to a degree that would impress a modern-day fetishist. In fact, gloves in the Victorian period were so skintight that ladies were unable to button their *mousquetaires* without assistance, hence the invention of the buttonhook! It was, in fact, considered improperly alluring for women to put on or entirely remove opera-length gloves in public, and several etiquette writers of the time advised women to put on their long gloves at home before venturing outdoors. The button- or snap-fastened wrist opening which is the characteristic feature of the *mousquetaire* was put to very good use in this respect by many ladies of the period, who would slip their hands out through the opening to eat or drink while keeping the glove itself on. Harrison Fisher's painting of a young woman at tea demonstrates this custom in action.

A young lady takes her hand out of her opera glove through the wrist opening
while having her tea, illustrated by Harrison Fisher

The kid opera glove has become one of the items of clothing, next to the button-up shoe, that is most associated with the elegance of the late Victorian and Edwardian eras. Currently, though, long white opera gloves are most closely associated with Kate Winslett's role in the 1997 movie "Titanic." She wears kidskin opera gloves during a key dinner scene in the film.

During the Napoleonic/Regency period, women's long gloves were tailored to fit loosely on the wearer's arm, and often worn gathered below the the elbow or helped up on the biceps with a garter-like strap. The Napoleonic/Regency glove style is well-demonstrated by Jacqueline Bisset as Josephine in the 1987 TV miniseries. Napoleonic and Regency, as this period was called in England; was the era Jane Austen wrote about, and ladies wearing long gloves are often to be seen in films made of her books, such as "Sense and Sensibility" and "Emma." Gloves were made of many materials and in bewildering variety of colors. Kidskin and cloth were favored materials, and the gloves were often made so that they fitted loosely around the wearer's arm and could be "scrunched" down toward the wrist at the wearer's option. In 2005, in the film version of "Pride and Prejudice," Rosamund Pike and several other actresses wear opera-length gloves with drawstring ties at the top of the glove. It is not an accurate representation of the style of long gloves at the Regency era. Fashion plates from this period do not show gloves with drawstring-type ties, but demonstrate women wearing gloves held up by garter-like straps or ribbons.

In United States, Western lady's gloves for formal and semi-formal wear occasions come in three length: wrist or so called "matinee," elbow, and opera or full-length (over the elbow, reaching the biceps.) There are expensive custom-made evening or opera gloves that are made from kid leather, also known as kidskin. Many other types of leather, most usually soft varieties of cowhide or deerskin, are used in making full-length gloves. Patent leather and suede are especially popular as alternatives to kidskin, and are often more affordable than kidskin. Latex or rubber opera gloves, most often used in latex and PVC fetishism are also available. Satin and stretch satin materials are extremely popular in mass production. Some women continue to wear gloves as a part of dress outfits, for example, for church and weddings. Long white gloves are common accessories for teenage girls attending such events as proms, debutante balls or formal ceremonies at church such as confirmation.

While the etymology of the term "opera gloves" is unknown, gloves of above-the-elbow length have been worn since at least the late 18th century, and gloves reaching to or just below the elbow have been worn by women in Western countries since the 17th century. There is an engraving of England's Queen Mary dating from the 1690s in which she is shown wearing elbow-length gloves.

Queen Mary II with mantilla, fan, and white elbow-length gloves, 1690

Queen Elizabeth I of England is reported as wearing an 18-inch-long pair of white leather gauntlets, with two inches of gold fringe, at a ceremony at Oxford in 1566. (Severn, p. 34) Some hundred years later, England's Queen Mary was painted in a portrait wearing a pair of elbow-length gloves.

Over-the-elbow gloves were widely popular during the Regency/Napoleonic period (circa 1800-1825), and continued the popularity during the early and mid-Victorian periods (circa 1830-1870), but enjoyed their greatest vogue in the last two decades of the 19th century and the years of the 20th century prior to start of World War I. During this period of time, opera gloves were a standard accessory for both daytime and evening wear with any type of outfits including swimwear.

Etiquette of that period considered gloves to be a mandatory accessory for both women and men of upper classes. Basically, it was fairly uncommon during this era to see a well-dressed woman at a public occasion who was not wearing gloves of some sort. In the late 19th century, the famous French actress, "the Divine Sarah," Sara Bernhardt, who liked wearing long gloves to disguise, what she considered, her overly thin arms. They also enhanced her expressive mannerism of hand movements on stage and her overall costumes' impact from the stage to the big screen. Sarah Bernardt introduced opera gloves to American ladies.

Sarah Bernhardt wears elbow-length white mousquetaire gloves in one of her roles

Lillian Russell, the famous New York actress and society beauty of the fin-de-siecle period, was known for her huge glove collection, especially for her shoulder-length gloves, and was often photographed wearing them. She caused a sensation when she rode along New York's Fifth Avenue on a gold and silver bicycle wearing white, shoulder-length kid gloves.

Lillian Russell wearing fingerless white kid opera gloves

The illustrations of Charles Dana Gibson, Henry Hutt, and Harrison Fisher are full with pictures of beautiful ladies wearing kidskin opera gloves, almost universally white. White, and its related colors, such as ivory, was considered the proper colors for gloves for any formal occasion for many decades. Black was considered a "daring" color, and opera gloves in other colors do not really seem to have started showing up until the 1920's or 1930's. Fisher, in particular, delighted in painting portraits of beautiful women in long gloves, as can be seen from this fine example of a sympathetic young lady.

"A young woman in opera gloves" by Harrison Fisher

Since World War I, opera gloves were the staple fashion accessory in the 1940s through the early 1960s. Hollywood costumes were seldom made to be worn. At times, they seem to be made only for posing. In reality, according to Diana Vreeland, "Hollywood was the world's back porch." "Whoever you were, a secretary in Bavaria, a housewife in South Dakota, you went to the movies." The essence of the movies influences created the magic fashioned by Hollywood costume designs and its glamorous accessories. Adrian, Travis Banton, Helen Rose, Jean Luis knew how to pay the attention to finishing details by bringing to life the MGM motto – "Make it big! Does it right! Give it class!"

Most flapper costumes came complete with satin opera gloves, a confusing addition because flappers are most often seen with bear arms or light crocheted gloves which were popular during the 1920's.

Retro Fashion Accessory Prints: Hansen Gloves - Vintage Advertisement 1950s Print - 15.6'x11.7' by Vinmag

Today's textile collectors, specializing in gloves are spoiled by the choices. While opera gloves from all eras are an established collectible, can be picked up for as little as $10.00 per pair. Couture examples, like Schiaparelli's surrealist designs of the 1930s, or Christian Lacroix's more recent *trompe l-oeil* pieces will cost considerably more.

The Italian designer Elsa Schiaparelli created wearable art with her cutting edge fashion. She entered the fashion scene with the encouragement of Paul Poiret and began by designing knitwear. She was the rival of Coco Chanel during the 1930s when they designed for women between the two world wars; but their styles allowed them to serve very different women from the risk-takers to the classicists.

In the vintage fashion arena, gloves are inexpensive entrée. The early examples from prestigious Trefousee Company along with bear labels like Armani, Chanel, and St. Laurent are readily available. The Mobile Millinery Museum is a home to several hundred pair of vintage fashion gloves which are used on a regular base to complement the other costume collection items.

(On Left) Gloves with painted nail effect made from snakeskin (c.1935)

(On Right) "The Circus Collection" by Elsa Schiaparelli (c.1937). The image of Elsa's fashion accessory is from the Philadelphia Museum of Art's exhibit, curator Dilys E. Blum

This pair of evening gloves was worn with Elsa Schiaparelli's 'Tears' dress. Their strong pink color would have complemented the pink and magenta print of the dress. Schiaparelli had a knack for taking everyday garments and using unusual details and trimmings to make them extraordinary. Here, instead of a traditional glove-leather, a pink crêpe fabric is used. Crêpe was stretchier, precluding the need for buttons or fastenings. The dramatic shirred ruffles which run the entire length of each glove provide an additional unexpected touch.

During the 1940's, after the war was over, glamorous opera gloves came back into style. Opera gloves remain popular in mid-century. Sadly, after WWII Elsa Schiaparelli was unable to continue designing since the direction of the fashion world was changing so much. But her artistic spirit lives on with the help of modern designers like Dolce & Gabbana. They think pink or orange to get us dressed for tomorrow...

In 1950s, gloves were "the order of the day." Gloves were worn everywhere to complete a woman's grooming. Without gloves the woman was not properly accessorized. Gloves were the hallmark of a lady, and white and creams were the most favored colors. Gloves were usually made of cotton as this was more affordable than leather gloves or the newer nylon material. Many women would own a special pair of leather gloves. They were sometimes referred to as 1950s Gauntlet Gloves. Dents and Pittards were popular glove-names as well. Women could make their own gloves using such as McCall's pattern listed at http://www.anothertimevintageapparel.com

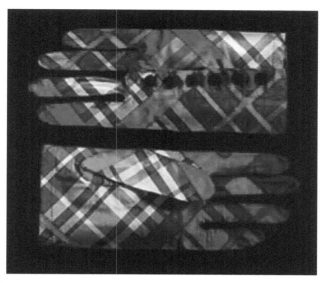

Checked gloves, 1930s. Note: There are over 500 pairs of gloves in the Fashion Museum collection.

While the wearing of gloves, as an indispensable part of a woman's outfit, fell into desuetude during the 1960's, opera gloves still pop up whenever a woman wants to look elegant or sexy. Most recently, for example, country singer Shania Twain set the 1999 Grammy awards ceremony on its ear when she performed in an outfit that included shoulder-length, fringed black opera gloves.

The formality of wearing gloves even continued into the sixties with popular stretch nylon and designed almost like a golfing glove. By the 1970s, gloves were more used functionally for keeping the hands warm than for any other reason.

In popular culture, there are the best known images incorporated the opera gloves by Rita Hayworth in "Gilda" (1946) and Marilyn Monroe in "Gentlemen Prefer Blondes" (1953.) Actress Audrey Hepburn was also known for glove wearing on and off screen. She also wore short gloves on her real wedding day, and this deserves a post on its own.

 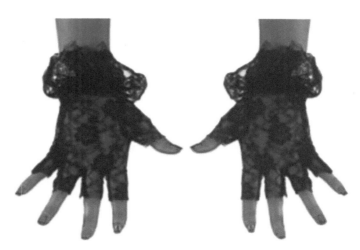

In the 80's, lace gloves were popularized by Madonna in "desperately seeking" Susan. Fingerless gloves were also popular during this time. Appreciatively, the combination of these trends is mostly left to Halloween costumes and 80's theme parties.

In 1992, Geena Davis wowed the 1992 Academy Awards with an outfit that included gleaming white satin opera gloves that went literally all the way up to the shoulder. Sarah Ferguson carried on the grand tradition of elegance and romance by wearing opera gloves at the 2004 Golden Awards show. Who can forget the iconic photos of movie stars such as Grace Kelly and Ava Gardner wearing glamorous opera-length gloves? The photos of a demure Princess Grace or impeccable Jackie Kennedy wearing short, white, and pristine gloves also became iconic. Grace Kelly was so much associated with white gloves that it was apparently possible to tell that an occasion was elegant when she changed into long ones! Gina Lollobrigida, Marilyn Monroe, Vivien Leigh, Jayne Mansfield, Natalie Wood, Joan Collins, Rita Hayworth, Morgan Fairchild, Loni Anderson, Pamela Anderson Lee, Shannen Doherty, Deborah Duchene, Phoebe Cates, Famke Janssen, Kate Winslett, Kay Kendall, Carmen Electra, Samantha Fox, Billie Burke, Yvonne De Carlo, Carole Landis, Gypsy Rose Lee, Jane Wyman, Barbara Stanwyck, Dorothy Lamour, Paulette Goddard, Stephanie Beacham, and many, many others wearing - what else? - opera gloves and other long gloves. Long gloves were an important accessory of Christian Dior's "New Look" designs. Women, who wanted to add a particular elegant touch to their formal outfits, enjoyed minor revivals in fashion design on several occasions in recent years, for example, in his *haute couture* in fall/winter collection of 2007.

The opera glove has been recognized for well over a century as one of the leading symbols of feminine elegance and sensuality. The very sight of a kidskin, suede, satin or lame glove that is embracing the hand and arm of a woman; sends a powerful conscious and subconscious signal that the wearer is a woman of style, elegance, passion, power, and sexuality. To this day, it is mandatory for female participants at the Vienna Opera Ball to wear white opera gloves.

President of the United States Gerald Ford, First Lady Betty Ford, Japanese Emperor Hirohito, and Empress Consort Nagako during a state dinner in 1975

In the same time, controversially, there has been a sharp decline in the use of gloves as fashion accessories over past several decades. Fewer and fewer girls attend their proms with gloves. Although, female dress is not as formally codified as that of men, where white tie is prescribed women and generally expected from them to wear full-length dresses such as ball gowns. Depending on the formality of the event, bare shoulders may or may not be acceptable. Shawls and long gloves are common accessories. At the most formal balls, ball gowns are often required to be white.

Fashion is always comes and goes in circles, and only time will tell the future developments of the trends of gloves. More than a century ago, Mary Todd Lincoln was criticized for her own fashion obsession – the gloves. Observers noted that in one four-month period she bought more than 400 pairs of this fashion accessory on her frequent buying trips to New York. And if Michelle Obama's shoe-matching apple-green inauguration gloves are an indication of future American fashion trend, gloves will be the new hot accessory. For good reason, as the first African American First Lady, she is writing her own rules, establishing a new etiquette, and changing the definition of what it means to be a woman in America today.

First Lady, Michelle Obama accessorized the dress with unusual green gloves from J. Crew and green shoes

There is a legend that gloves became fashionable amongst the nobility in Italy, in 1071, when the Doge of Venice, Domenico Seivo, married a well-dressed Constantine who liked wearing them. The aristocracy favored beautiful decorated gloves that were often adorned with jewels or embroidery and made of fine materials such as leather or fur. Monarchs also favored scented gloves, a practice that began in Italy. According to a rumor, Catherine de Medici's perfumer, Rene de Florentin, put scent on the gloves to hide the smell of the poisonous potions that she used to murder her many enemies. It is probably more of a truth that she just disliked the smell of her leather gloves. Catherine is supposed to have introduced perfumed gloves to France. Perfumes used to scent gloves included ambergris, civet, and musk.

The fashionable accessory has been fascinated wearers for centuries, although some types of gloves were banned in European countries by sumptuary laws. There were laws preventing the wearing of certain clothing and accessories by "commoners" to prevent extravagance and vanity. Rome, for example, banned perfumed gloves in 1560.

Jumping from history to present, the stylish accessory has been a comeback recently. The fall fashion shows featured gloves of all shapes and materials. These include pretty lace ones, long leather gloves, and even, opera gloves. Layered ones, especially useful to keep the cold away, are colorful as well. Italian glove-makers have always been highly regarded because of the quality of their materials and craftsmanship. Sermonetta and Gallo are some of the better known brands to choose from, if somebody is interested in buying these accessories for the winter. Gloves could be a part of wearable art. Nobody can forget the Dolce & Gabbana's hat and scarf set made out of black-and-white gloves worn by Elsa.

In Japan, ladies wear long gloves all day in summer to protect the ideal *irojiro* or fear skin as it represents beauty, grace, and high social status. Many Japanese ladies avoid any form of tanning due to the culture believe of purity and divinity in local religions. The everlasting Sailor Moon's gloves are opera length. The most common materials are latex and PVC fetishism.

In Germany, both latex and PVC fetishism are very common. Susan Wayland is one of many latex fetish models. Many women and men wear latex opera gloves.

In the Fall 2009 – Winter 2010 fashion season, gloves themselves were a hot trend, and many fashion designers paid lots of attention to them. Gloves certainly add much sophistication and glamour to outfits. Leather gloves are always in style. They are classic, and if you want to have a pair to be appropriated now and ten years later, this is exactly what you need. Besides, there are various designs to choose from such as Chado Ralph Rucci, Zac Posen, Thakoon, and Fendi. Derek Lam suggested reptile leather to make gloves from.

Women's leather gloves are the dictum of fashion. With black leather gloves you are the "thing!" Leather gloves make you a model, even when you aren't. Even, if you do not know your size, leather is forgiving. It is after all, skin. Leather gloves are a great gift because they adjust. Little small or big in size: not a problem. In fitting a glove, it's all about the span of the palm. Tight or not? Too tight means a too small palm. A lot of wrinkles means too big. Leather gloves will eventually fit the palm you buy them for. A gift that may work in to be the best thing you've ever gotten or given. Why buy them as a gift? Leather keeps out wind and cold. It was made to do that. Leather will adjusts, as any skin, because it was made to do that. Given a choice, buy leather. It is ecological, and it looks good, too. Leather gloves are fashionable and politically correct, and a match made in heaven!

Suede gloves aren't as practical as leather ones, but they do look beautiful. Ralph Lauren offers classic styles, while Carolina Herrera and Derek Lam give details to street-like casual style.

Velvet gloves always add chic to any wardrobe. They are elegant and sexy, and they are appropriate for different occasions.

Satin gloves are made from smooth and shinning fabric, and they are good with both evening gowns and denim combination. Lace gloves are very tender and cute in the same time. Some are made from a quite sheer fabric, others are lightly patterned. Short mannish gloves are new items for the girls who do not like feminine items.

White cotton gloves are good for many different social functions such as weddings, funerals, or at the flag bearer ceremony. Although white cotton gloves are used for multitasking purposes – can be worn as server's gloves for waiters and waitresses at a formal dinner; can be worn in a receiving line, can be used for entertaining by clowns or magicians. Sometimes, the white cotton gloves are worn at special functions by patriotic organizations such as the Daughters of the

American Revolution, American Legion Auxiliary and the Colonial Dames XVII, etc. White cotton parade gloves are made from 100% cotton; slip-on style without ornamental stitching. They are widely used by bands, in church, at banquets, by doormen, by military personal, by Santa Clauses and various uniformed men and women.

Knitted gloves are warm and cozy for the cold winter season to keep the ladies hands happy and pretty. Arm warmers (or arm socks) are knitted "sleeves" worn on the arms. Usually worn by dancers to warm up their bodies before class, they became brand new fashion items. Various sub-cultures, such as the punk, the emo, and the Goth subcultures, have also adopted arm warmers as a fashion statement. Such stores as Hot Topic and others sell arm warmers with chains and designs of skulls, piano keys and other alternative inspired designs. For the 2010 FIFA World Cup, arm warmers became a phenomenon in the host country of South Africa and abroad, too.

Style tip note: How cold weather accessory add instant chic to your outfit? With the glove. Fall 2010's runways demonstrated a versatile variety of gloves, both short and long. How to integrate gloves into your cold weather wardrobe? Specialists in the field advise to try long, above-the-elbow length gloves with a floor length gown for glamour. Knit fingerless gloves for a bit of sporty action are in, or even puffer gloves, juxtaposed against something feminine, to protect you from the cold winter.

A distinctive theme that exists for the fall and winter season's gloves boasts that there are wonderfully unique choices for just about every age, taste and budget. The season's most elegant lace, satin, sheer tulle, silk, fishnet or velvet await weddings, cocktail parties and other evening or formal events. Chenille, polyesters and cotton knits offer classic comfort for casual outdoor occasions such as sporting events, or simply taking a refreshing walk in the crisp cool air of autumn. Trims such as funky animal prints and festive fringe embellish some of the most contemporary glove styles. Elegant beads, feminine embroidered flowers, faux pearls, sparkly sequins, crystals and fun furs adorn many of the more sophisticated glove styles. In addition to traditional black, brown and white gloves, exciting hues such as emerald green, purple, red and metallic gold and silver eagerly await the glove connoisseur for the impending any holiday season!

The major mass production companies that are manufacturing leather gloves are located in India, Pakistan and China. Expensive women's fashion gloves are made in France, Canada and other countries. For cheaper male gloves New York State, especially Gloversville, New York, is a center of glove manufacturing. However, more and more glove manufacturing is being done in East Asia.

Carolina Herrera came out with elegant embroidered gloves for the Fashion Week Fall 2011. Marc Jacobs' ensemble of yellow gloves at Mercedes-Benz Fashion Show Week in Fall 2009 was a memorable event. Ralph Lauren' lined leather gloves for $50-$100 are a luxurious accessory. DKNY has an impressive collection of fall/winter wool gloves for men from sued to peacoat.

The gloves above are available at net-a-porter.com, ASOS.com, blackbirdballard.com, and oasis-stores.com

What about the young generation of fashion designers' of gloves? One of the premier accessory designers in the country, Carolina Amato, has been at the helm of the luxury accessories company that bears her name for more than thirty years. She is a New York-based designer. Her signature label gloves, hats, scarves, wraps and other accessories for men and women can be found in the most prestigious department and specialty stores through the U.S. as well as England, Japan, Canada and South Korea. Her designs are regularly featured in top fashion magazines such as *Vogue, Elle, W, Harpers Bazaar, Town & Country and Vanity Fair,* to name just a few. A graduate of Ohio University, where she graduated with a Bachelor's Degree in Fine Arts; Ms. Amato originally intended to be a painter. She was praised for her early work by colleagues who often cited her technique with strong, playful combinations of color, patterns, and unique talent that would serve her well when she eventually turned her creative energies to fashion and accessories design. Perhaps not so coincidentally, Ms. Amato hails from a family of Italian textile professionals, a legacy that began with both her maternal and paternal grandmothers, each of whom were skilled craftswomen who plied their craft in New York's garment center. Her grandfather made his living as a furniture upholsterer, and the designer recalls her childhood "filled with days spent playing with the multicolored ribbons, trims, and fine fabrics from her grandparents' workshops." As a young woman, she learned to sew on her grandmother's sewing machine, an experience she would take with her and utilize as she entered the creative world of fashion and textile design.

Rather than apprentice to a working designer, Ms. Amato jumped head first into the fashion business, establishing Carolina Amato, Inc.; her own accessories design company, in 1979, with a small loan from her husband. Today, Carolina Amato enjoys a huge and loyal following among such upscale retailers as Neiman Marcus, Anthropologie, Lord & Taylor and Saks Fifth Avenue, along with style-conscious consumers who appreciate the impeccable Italian workmanship, consistent fit and fashionable design of her accessories. From soft and plush cashmere knits and "pop-top" fingerless mittens, to over the elbow silk charm use gauntlets and her new, trend-setting "ultra luxe" Italian leather collection, Carolina Amato's richly colored and textured collections cover most fashion bases, from the trendy to the timeless. For her line of men's gloves, the designer regularly focuses on elegant ribbed cashmere, buttery Italian leather, shearling and the softest suede. One of the hottest items: cropped perforated leather driving gloves that feel right at home behind the wheel of a sporty BMW roadster or a Mercedes Benz coupe. An active member of the Council of Fashion Designers of America (CFDA) for nearly two decades, Ms. Amato has also served on the organization's Scholarship Committee, which endows funds toward the education of promising young fashion designers. She continues to serve as a panel judge for the Savannah College of Art and Design's annual Student Fashion Show and sits on the Parents Council of the prestigious Rhode Island School of Design (RISD). Ms. Amato has also been a member of the Accessories Council (AC) for several years now.

When she is not working on the design of her numerous collections, Ms. Amato enjoys cooking in her Tuscan-inspired kitchen, entertaining friends and family at her home on the north shore of Long Island, skiing in Vermont, and traveling regularly to Italy with her husband, the celebrated architect Frank Capone.

Carolina Amato, Accessory Designer and Expert

2011 fall's polka-dot trends or "going dotty" occupied the fashion design and home décor from Barneys New York polka-dot folding umbrella to Marc Jacobs' nylon polka-dot tights. Playful pair of polka-dot crochet gloves by Carolina Amato covered in dash of dots is an adorable take on an uber-ladylike accoutrement. Cotton gloves are available at BHLDN in black and white motif, one size fit all.

Meantime, *"LaCrasia Duchein has made them* [gloves] *the hottest item in fashion..."* According the LaCrasia Gloves web site information, a FIT graduate, LaCrasia Lorne Duchein had a vision

"to reclaim the fame of gloves and bring them back as a women's wardrobe staple."

LaCrasia is an ultimate destination for glove production. Started at 1973 as a belt designer, she is designing and manufacturing hand wear since 1978. LaCrasia offers a retail outlet and web site that features gloves in rainbow of colors for both men and women. The wholesale division provides bulk orders as well as private label collections. The stylist closet contains over 6, 000 pairs of fashion glove rentals for advertising campaigns. If the perfect glove is not available on display, LaCrasia will gladly fashion a custom-made pair. LaCrasia.com is a new interactive web site for easy worldwide access to her ever-changing offerings of fun ways to dress up the hand. An online catalogue shows you a view of the wonderful world of LaCrasia's gloves which can fulfill any basic needs, most personal requirements, or even any wildest fantasies.

Below is a listing of bibliography from LaCrasia Gloves web site that speaks for itself.

New York Times "Special Fall Fashion Issue" by Kathy Horn, 3 August, 2007. Please see article at: http://www.nytimes.com/pages/fashion/index.html?th&emc=th
"Zagat Survey" - 2007 New York City Shopping Guide - page 158

"LaCrasia Gloves" *1181 Broadway 8th floor, New York, NY 10001 (B'way & W 28th Street) m N/R/W to 28 St. 212-803-1600*

"Your fingers can find fashionable coverage all year round" at this "great focused resource" on the fringes of the Flatiron District offering every "glove you can imagine" from "arm-length" numbers "for that black-tie outfit" to "racy fine leather driving" styles; hand mavens vow "this place is a trip, even if your digits don't need protection."

"Where to Wear 2006." - New York Shopping Guide, page 164

"Nothing brings a tear to the eye of nostalgia's like the memory of our once great glove trade... Enter LaCrasia Gloves, who have been in the business since 1973. They will customize any glove to any hand. Just send in a tracing" [of your hand, the type you did as a kid when readying to draw turkeys.]

"Metro Holiday Gift Guide," 7 December, 2006

"We've got to hand it to LaCrasia (wegloveyou.com), one of the few shops in the country that still custom-cut men's and women's gloves...We're sure you'll give it the thumbs up."

New York Magazine, 2 February, 2004

"LaCrasia has any type of glove you can think of, including kid gloves in all lengths and colors, because they are one of the premier glove makers in the fashion industry."

"Romantic Victorian Weddings Then and Now"

"LaCrasia is the 'First Name' in wholesale custom gloves."

F.I.T. Network, Winter 2000

"Brides, wrestlers, debutantes, strippers, military men, Las Vegas showgirls, race car drivers, Hollywood actors, The Rockettes, and riot police are among the clientele of LaCrasia Gloves, one of the few remaining custom "glovers" in the world."

Robb Report, December 2000

"When Mr. Ruckel (at LaCrasia Gloves) hangs up his cutting shears, it may well be the last stitch in time for the long white leather debutante glove made in America."

Diane Sawyer, ABC-TV, Good Morning America, 30 April, 1999

"LaCrasia Gloves are the only gloves worth having. Just ask Jackie Kennedy, Carolina Herrera, Donna Karan, Geoffrey Beene, Madonna, Sylvester Stallone, Prince, Brooke Shields, Michael Jackson, Michelle Pfeiffer and others, not to mention entire casts of Broadway shows, and almost all the Seventh Avenue show designers."

Accessories Magazine, May 1996

"Today LaCrasia Duchein has a corner on the American market because, for one, her gloves are assembled from start to finish in one of the last glove manufacturing plants in the United States."

The Cleveland Plain Dealer, 1 November, 1990

"Glove Story: How LaCrasia Duchein has made them the hottest item in fashion…It was LaCrasia Duchein, who had made up her mind to bring gloves back from oblivion…People still find it hard to believe that she doesn't have her gloves made in the Philippines, but for LaCrasia it's a joy and a necessity to be around the machinery, and the men who make them; and she is determined to keep fine glove making alive in America."

Fashion maverick, designer and artist, Daphne Guinness, is a work of art herself. The diamond-encrusted glove she made with the jeweler Shaun Leane is one of the latest contemporary novelties. Currently, New York City is seeing traces of Daphne Guinness. She is one of the unnamed models used by her friend David LaChapelle in new photographic works on display at the Lever House Art Collection. In the Metropolitan Museum, right opposite her apartment building, there is a major exhibition of work by another designer, the late Alexander McQueen, featuring many dresses from Guinness's own collection. Her extraordinary couture collection was exhibited at New York's Fashion Institute of Technology in September of 2011.

She is writing a novel, she is painting, and she has just finished three films. Two are by her friend the photographer Joe Lally, and she produced them as well as acts in them. She has also directed her own short films, and *Cashback*, the film she produced for the photographer Sean Ellis, was nominated for an Oscar in 2004. Guinness has her finger in so many creative things that it is hard to know how to describe her: artist, actress, heiress, patron, muse, and collector, and model, and designer. What she is, most of all is something so rare these days that we tend to dismiss it as eccentricity: a woman who is always uniquely, authentically herself. With her striking badger-stripe hair and her quirky mix of couture, vintage and self-designed clothes, Guinness is a true original.

In England, Dents designers continue distinguished heritage producing the finest leather gloves. The history of Dents can be traced back to 1777, when John Dent established his accessory company manufacturing fine leather gloves in Worcester, England.

The historic facts that are tracing the benchmark's of Dents' glove-making could be found at the Dents website at http://www.dents.co.uk

Dents, Fairfield Road Warminster, Wiltshire, England BA12 9DL. Telephone: +44 (0) 1985 212291 fax: +44 (0) 1985 216435
E-mail: dents@dents.co.uk Visit our website www.dents.co.uk

Many of Dents' accessories are handmade using

Printed in England

John Dent's sons, John Jr. and William, served seven-year apprenticeship's beginning at the age of fifteen. It was their partnership that made Dent's famous around the world. In the nineteenth century, the company expanded rapidly and had subsidiaries everywhere from Sydney to New York and to Prague. In the twentieth century, it made the gloves for both George VI and Elizabeth II on their coronations. At Dents' glove making never really underwent a mechanization phase, unlike most industries in the nineteenth century. While most gloves today are made in Asia on a vast scale, original makers like Dents still use hand cutting and individual judgment to get the models right. Tailoring, the glove-cutting, is the most important process as the person who cuts the shape by hand and ensures the shape and fit are correct. The cutting is done around card patterns that date back to 1845 and come in twenty different sizes.

THE CRAFT OF GLOVEMAKING

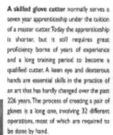

A skilled glove cutter normally serves a seven year apprenticeship under the tuition of a master cutter. Today the apprenticeship is shorter, but it still requires great proficiency borne of years of experience and a long training period to become a qualified cutter. A keen eye and dexterous hands are essential skills in the practice of an art that has hardly changed over the past 226 years. The process of creating a pair of gloves is a long one, involving 32 different operations, most of which are required to be done by hand.

Using a "donkey" frame to hold the glove while it is being sewn. Dents factory circa 1900.

The finest leathers

The natural qualities of leather, with its subtle variation and nuances of shading and occasional marking, tests the skill of Dents leather buyers and selectors, because no two pieces of leather are ever the same. To select the perfect leather for each style of glove, every individual piece of leather must be carefully sorted, inspected and graded, and no machine can match the selector's skill and knowledge. The experienced eye of the leather selector recognises the wide variety of different leathers, with variation in grain, texture, thickness and strength. All of these qualities must be assessed before selecting that one special piece that is uniquely suitable for the particular glove being created. It is this constant search for perfection, and commitment to quality, which gives a Dents glove that "secret fit" and comfort that is its hallmark.

Dents factory seamstress, circa 1892.

Crafted with skill and pride

Today, each pair of Dents gloves is crafted with loving care by craftspeople whose attention to the smallest detail creates a glove that is a unique and timeless accessory.

This tradition of craftsmanship is embodied in Dents' commitment to preserving the revered skills and craftsmanship of its founder, John Dent.

Gloving Punch, as used for over 200 years.

Cutting shears and glove stretchers

Cutting the leather – the "secret fit"

When selecting a pair of gloves, the most important consideration, apart from the beauty of the leather, is the fit. One of the best-loved features of any Dents glove is its special fit, and this is owed entirely to the skill and experience of the master cutter. The cutter's keen eye, borne of years of experience, together with the careful shaping and stretching of leather, will influence the final fit of the glove.

The style and design of the glove will be determined by the glove "pattern". This is a flat, thick piece of card in the shape of a glove. A different pattern is required for each individual size, and will vary according to the type of leather being used. All high-quality gloving leathers have a natural stretch, and the pattern must be adjusted according to the stretch required, to ensure a perfect fitting glove.

The patterns used today date back to 1839 and are available in 20 different sizes. Prior to circa 1845, all gloves were sewn by hand because there was no machinery available to help the craftspeople. Today at Dents, many gloves are still sewn by hand, but the wooden "donkey" is no longer used as a guide for the stitching, and the skilled hand-sewer stitches freehand. It was not until after 1845, with the invention of the Elias Howe machine, that mechanical sewing was introduced into glovemaking.

Finishing touches

It is now time for the back of the glove to be decorated. Today, the traditional classic three rows of stitching, known as "points", are most common, although in the past it was not unusual to decorate the backs of gloves or cuffs with embroidery. Nowadays, it is more likely to be a fancy stitch, button, brass or metal detail trimming that decorates the back of the glove.

The lining of any glove is very important, and the care with which the lining is made and inserted will affect the glove's final appearance. A glove may be lined with a variety of materials, silk and cashmere being the most popular linings used today. A Dents glove lining is actually made as a separate glove and, when inserted into the glove, effectively becomes a glove within another glove. This gives an improved fit, and makes the gloves more comfortable to wear.

The different parts of the glove are now ready to be assembled and stitched together by machine or by hand. Gloves can be stitched in a variety of ways, depending on the weight of the leather and the lining being used. Every method of stitching has its own special name. The Prickseam method, whereby the two edges of the gloves are exposed, is used for heavier weight leathers, whereas Inseam is, as the name suggests, a method by which the gloves are stitched inside out so, when they are finally turned the right way out, the

Sewing the "points" on the back of the glove. Only the hand and eye of the skilled machinist ensures accuracy. Dents factory, Warminster, England.

inseam stitch becomes invisible, leaving a neat seam.

The glove is now ready for the separate glove lining to be inserted by hand using a Lining Former, which is the traditional method used by Dents. The gloves are now nearly complete, except that they must be carefully ironed. This process was originally known as Laying-out, and was done entirely by hand with the aid of Dolly sticks, which were inserted into the gloves with a damp cloth. Today, gloves are ironed on an electrically heated brass hand to give them their special finished appearance. This process is still known as Laying-out.

It takes 32 different operations to make a pair of Dents gloves and, as each operation is complete, they are carefully examined for any imperfections which, if found, will result in their immediate rejection. Only then will the gloves be deemed worthy to carry the famous Dents label, and to be finally passed for shipment to a Dents appointed retailer.

Dents exhibition stand, circa 1919.

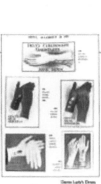

Dents Ladies' Dress Gloves, circa 1930.

Left: Inserting the glove lining, using a Lining Former. Dents factory, Warminster, England.

Measurements and Sizes, Patterns and Production, and *"The Etiquette of Opera Gloves"*

The length of ladies' evening gloves is measured in terms of "buttons," whether they, in fact, have buttons or not. The word is derived from French. Wrist length gloves are usually eight-button long, those at the elbow are 16, mid-biceps are 22 and full shoulder-length are 30. Opera gloves are between 16 and 22 inches long, some gloves can be as long as 29 or 30 inches, as one-button size is a bit longer than one inch. A petite woman might have a smaller size, while a tall woman might need a glove longer than 22 inches. The glove shorter than elbow-length should not be referred to as an opera glove under any circumstances. When ordering gloves, measurements should be taken around the hand at the fullest portion of the palm:

For hand size	Order glove size
7" to 8"	Small
8" to 9"	Medium
9" to 10"	Large
10" to 11"	X-Large

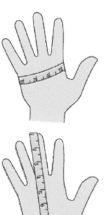

A) Measure around the hand at the fullest part (exclude thumb)

B) Measure from the tip of the middle finger to the base of the hand

C) Use the larger of these two measurements for the correct size glove

D) If you are right-handed, take measurements from your right hand

E) If you are left-handed, take measurements from your left hand

F) The number of inches measured equals the size of the glove
(For example, 7" measurement equals a size 7 glove)

During history, there have been varied sumptuary laws regarding the use of colors, materials and decorations of glove. Customs also controlled the use of gloves. One was - to remove gloves when in the presence of greeting people. This possibly led to a 15th century fashion of wearing only the left glove and wearing the right glove on the belt. Apparently, the giving of a poison glove as a gift to an enemy was also common in the 15th century, and beyond.

The first Glovers Guilds were recorded in the 14th century England. During the 16th century the number of Glovers Guilds increased. There are no found any published patterns prior to the 17th century. The main difference between modern patterns and the patterns from the *Le Gant*, which could be found on *The Glove Website* and *Didero*t patterns from 1800's, is the thumb.

As it is noticed before, during the 16th century, scented gloves were in fashion. This is documented in "Queen Elizabeth's Wardrobe Unlock'd" for Elizabethan and Spanish gloves. As the story goes, Duke of Oxford gave Queen Elizabeth a pair of Italian scented gloves. In the book "Queen Elizabeth's Wardrobe Unlock'd" is listed documentation for perfuming in 1563 such as fine carving tools to cut gloves; and descriptions on types of scents, and how they were applied.

They could be perfumed with *"of jessamine, ambergris, washed with malmsely wine and coated with a odiferous grease; powered of cypress, pomade, oil of cedar, oil of benzoin, grains of musk, cinnamon, closes storax, nutmeg, oil of lemon, civet, water of orange flowers, musk rose, goat tallow mixed with oil of jessamine, martells, lemon camphor, white lead, oil of sweet almonds, roots of white lily, rose water, oil of musk oil of fruit stone, white ambergris, oil of storax."* (Arnold, 1988, p. 217)

There are usually eight components of a leather glove: palm and back (one piece), thumb, three fourchettes (slender pieces of leather that form the sides of the fingers), and three quirks, or diamond-shaped pieces inserted at the bottom between the fingers. In cutting gloves, a single trank, or rectangular piece of leather the size of the glove, may be cut by hand to a desired pattern with shears; or a number of tranks may be cut simultaneously by a weighted, sharp steel die. The glove is closed by stitching up along the outside to the tip of the little finger; then the thumbs, quirks, and fourchettes are set in and sewed with great care. Although some sewing is done by hand, most is by machine and closely resembles hand stitching. The completed glove is dampened, tailored on an electrically heated metal model hand, and buffed.

Fabric gloves of antiquity were made of woven material, but modern fabric gloves are knit. Silk was the favored material before World War II, but the glove industry now relies on cotton and man-made fibers such as rayon and nylon. Glove-sized squares of finished fabric are arranged face-to-face, so that both left and right hands are cut out together by the knife-sharp glove die, which is forced through the built-up layers of fabric. Gores, triangular pieces of fabric, are cut separately and attached between the fingers when the cutout glove is folded over and stitched together. Thumbs are also cut separately and attached. The fingers are given a tubular shape by seaming. Fabric gloves are tailored on electrically heated metal hands, as are leather gloves.

Gloves of wool, synthetic fibers, and cotton yarns can be knit by machine with or without seams; and their colors, designs, patterns, and stitch variations rival those of gloves knit by hand. Seamed, or wrought, gloves are first machine knit as flat selvage pieces of fabric, folded, so that complementing parts fall together, and then stitched. Seamless gloves also may be knit entirely on a flat machine or the cuff and palm may be knit on a circular machine, and then the stitches carefully transferred to a flat fingering machine.

Protective gloves have been developed for special uses. Thin rubber or latex gloves are used by medical and laboratory personnel. Heavy rubber gloves are used by electrical workers. Asbestos gloves protect against burns, as do gloves of heavy, twisted loop pile similar to terry cloth. Canton flannel gloves treated with polyvinyl provide plastic-coated work gloves that are heat resistant, impermeable to most fluids, and proof against acids, alkalis, industrial oils, greases, and other chemicals. Lead-impregnated gloves may be used in order to shield the hands from X-rays.

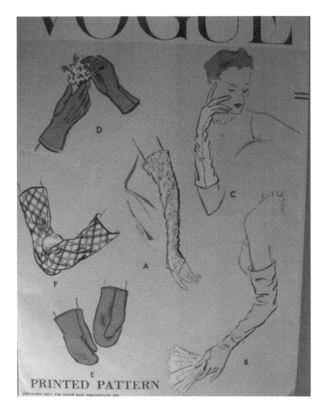

Glove glossary for pattern making or "the map of gloves"

Police officers often wear them to work in crime scenes to prevent destroying evidence in the scene. Many criminals wear gloves to avoid leaving fingerprints, which makes the crime investigation more difficult. However, not all gloves prevent fingerprints from being left on the crime scene, depending on the material from which the glove is made. For more information, please read "CSI Experience Forensic Science Service: Fingerprinting." Gloves and gauntlets are integral components of pressure suits and spacesuits such as the Apollo/Skylab A7L which went to the moon. Spacesuit gloves combine toughness and environmental protection with a degree of sensitivity and flexibility.

Today, special arthritis gloves may ease pain and stiffness in achy hands, fingers and wrists. Ultra-comfy stretch gloves provide soothing warmth and relief to sore and arthritic joints. According to the new scientific buzz, they help alleviate throbbing, tingling and swelling, too, and can be worn all day long, even in the sleep.

Glove-making is an old art and has some terms that may be unfamiliar to even the most passionate glove enthusiast:

- **Cabretta:** Thin, fine leather made from the skin of Brazilian hair sheep.
- **Cape or Capeskin:** Superior thin leather made from the skin of South African hair sheep.
- **Clute Cut:** A glove style with a one piece palm with no seam at the base of the finger. There are seams along the fingers on the inside.
- **Cuff:** The part of the glove extending up the arm, to lengthen the glove. This could be made separately, and in some cases, from differing materials. It can be very ornately decorated. It varied in length depending on the fashion.
- **Fourchette:** The piece of leather sewn between the fingers on some kinds of gloves. They could be made from long rectangular pieces of material, or this could be made of differing

materials, particularly for Elizabethan gloves; V-shaped, as in *Le Gant's* pattern. Fourchettes could be extended to lengthen the fingers. Some fashions were pointed at the tips.

• **Gauntlet:** A very long cuff to protect the forearm.

• **Grain:** The side of the leather that had the hair, i.e. the outside. Full grain has the original surface, whereas corrected grain has been abraded to make the leather smoother and more uniform.

• **Gunn Cut:** A glove style with seams at the base of the fingers. The seams between the fingers are on the back of the glove.

• **Gusset:** The piece of leather sewn between the fingers on some kinds of gloves. Also known as the sidewall or fourchette.

• **Quirk:** This is a small triangular gusset, sewn in at the base of the fourchettes, between the fingers and more commonly used in modern gloves. There is some evidence they were used in 17th century.

• **Split:** When a thick piece of leather is split into two thinner pieces, the top piece will have grain (top grain); and the bottom piece will be suede on both sides. The bottom piece is the split.

• **Trank:** Body of the glove, covering the palm area to the wrist.

• **Welt:** Thin piece of leather sewn into the seam to strengthen it. Often a welt is used in the seam at the crotch of the thumb and the base of the finger.

The Grandoe sports rich history of glove innovation is displayed for customers and tourists alike at the Grandoe Museum. Located in the center of glove-making history in Gloversville, NY, the museum tells the story of glove-making at Grandoe. Visitors can learn about glove manufacturing techniques, leathers processing, and glove styles from past years. With over 100 years of glove memorabilia, the Grandoe museum is a hidden gem and well worth the stop.

While visiting the museum, "glove-lovers" have the opportunity to browse the Grandoe factory store and find great deals on quality gloves.

The Grandoe Corporation, 11 Grandoe Lane, Gloversville, NY 12078 at Grandoe.com

From modest beginnings as leather-glove manufacturer in the late 1800's, Grandoe gloves has grown to become one of the premier winter sport glove brand. Their reputation as a leading producer of innovative and high quality products that enhance people's comfort dates back to their first glove patent in 1897, and it continues today. In fact, Grandoe gloves are proud to have more patented and patent-pending comfort technologies currently in use that are more than any other glove manufacturer in the business.

For more than 100 years Grandoe has been praised and honored for the special products it creates. At present, under the ownership and direction of the fourth and fifth generations of its founding family, Grandoe's strong tradition of producing the finest high performance ski, snowboard, and outdoor gloves has made it the number-one choice of Olympic ski and snowboard medalists, the U.S. National Freestyle Ski Team, and the multinational Trans-Antarctic Expedition. Leading winter sports and outdoor consumer publications have chosen Grandoe ski gloves to receive the "gold medal" award for outstanding product and have also paid tribute to Grandoe as the "warmest of the warm" in side-by-side comparison tests with other major glove brands. In the world of outdoor sports, Grandoe's mountaineering gloves are worn and endorsed by some of the most accomplished high altitude climbers, including world famous Ed Viesturs - the first American to climb the world's fourteen highest mountains (all with peaks over 8,000 meters above sea level) without supplemental oxygen.

According to Eric Friedman, Grandoe's President and CEO, *"What sets us apart from the competition is our selection of fine quality materials, attention to the smallest details including the latest color and styling trends, and the integration of exclusive comfort concepts that really make a difference in peoples' lives."* Grandoe glove productions are available in nearly every major market in the United States and in select markets around the world.

Gloves – Online, the GO Gloves, are the "glove gurus" in the premier international market for information about gloves. Gloves-Online showroom's specialty is on something unique and special, on "hard to find" gloves for individualized needs. The manufacturing engineers and glove technicians developed and manufactured gloves to meet modern specifications and requirements. As the GO's story goes, it was 1995, and the founder, Joe McGarry, was replying to customers' e-mail requests looking for gloves they couldn't find locally. These e-mail requests were a result of the Glove University that Joe created on his web site for his glove manufacturing business. The Glove University included glove facts, terms and information about glove styles and glove industry jargon. Joe McGarry discovered that there was no any major online retailer that specialized in gloves. So, in 1996, Joe decided to establish an online glove store, and Gloves-Online.com was born!

The original idea was to create a web site that offered the best selection of hard to find gloves based on the customers' e-mail requests. The first gloves to be offered were white parade type gloves, since these gloves were in high demand and were very difficult to locate.

Over the past decade, the Gloves-Online brand and their glove offerings have evolved into the largest full service on-line glove depot in terms of glove brands, styles, colors, sizes, and needs. GO's growth over years is largely responsible for their high level of customer service. The Gloves Online is one of the largest single source of glove suppliers in the world to retail consumers and industry. As Joe puts it, *"We currently sell gloves from Rawhide to Cashmere, and we have just begun. We want Gloves-Online to be known as a service company that happens to specialize in gloves."*

Stretch Freehands, gloves for iPhones and Cell Phones that help both to keep hands warm and stay mobile

The *"Pocket [Hand] Protector of the 21st Century"* blends fashion and function for *"texters,"* e-mail users on the go, gamers without removing the gloves. The combination of spandex nylon shell and micro-fleece lining keeps the hands warm, and the synthetic suede palm and fingers help to keep the grip. Any Freehands are great for winter outdoor activities.

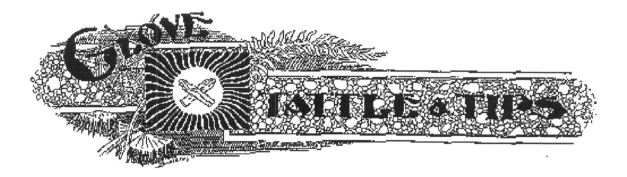

The glove industry of Fulton County, New York, could be watched at "The Glovers of Fulton County: A Documentary Video on-line." The Glove: Tattle & Tips sign is taken from a regular column in *Gloves* magazine, successor to *The Glovers' Review,* a monthly publication of the Glove Manufacturers Association that was scanned from the June 1937 issue.

Grandoe, GO Gloves, Wells Lamont, MAPA Gloves, Kinco, Youngstown, PIP, Freehands, Tempshield, MCR Safety, CarbonX, AmerCare, Ergodyne Gloves & Wrist Supports, Caiman Gloves are the major industrial brands. Glove brands help protect working hands and keep labor facilities running smoothly. Selected manufacturers ensure the highest levels of performance, safety, durability, value and fashion.

The Worshipful Company of Glovers of London, at www.thegloverscompany.org is one of the City's ancient Livery Companies, was formed originally to upkeep the standards of glove-making in the City some 700 years ago. In common with other City Livery Companies, the Glovers have survived and flourished by adapting to modern times, maintaining strong links with their trade, supporting the City with many of its projects, both educational and charitable programs.

The Spence and Harborow collections of gloves are housed at the Fashion Museum at Bath. (www.fashionmuseum.co.uk) These are two historic collections that are on loan to the Fashion Museum, a world class collection of contemporary and historical dress. The Glove Collection Trust has recently supported a special exhibition "17th Century Gloves" at the Fashion Museum with gloves from the Spence collection. The exhibition consists from an ongoing collection. Currently, the trustees are building the General Collection of gloves from the mid-19th Century to the present day. The web site contains some 265 pairs of gloves to date, acquired under their policy to collect gloves which illustrate the development of taste and fashion of gloves.

In 1959, the late Robert Spence presented his magnificent collection of historical gloves to the company. This Collection covers the period from the late 16th century until the middle of the 19th century, but its richest exhibits fall within the period of c.1590 and 1680. Spence obviously admired the splendidly decorated gauntlet gloves of the period and tried to assemble as wide a variety as possible. The combination of fine doeskin or kid gloves, with their narrow attenuated fingers and the richly embroidered gauntlet seemed to have exerted a special fascination for him, as it still does for enthusiasts today. Such gloves were the finest example of the work of two City Companies, the Glovers and Broderers. The embroidery incorporated multicolored silks, gold thread, seed pearls and applied metal strip sometimes worked on satin, and sometimes worked directly on to the leather. The majority of pairs used popular motifs of the period, flowers, leaves, birds and beasts, but some actually tell a story as does the pair which, in embroidery, depicts the allegory of Jonah and the Whale. Such splendid gloves were popular presents, and there are many references to them in household and royal accounts of the period of time in history. Occasionally, they served as a cover for even richer gifts. Sir Thomas More, as Chancellor, was given as a New Year present, by a lady in whose favor he had settled a legal dispute, a pair of gloves containing forty angels (an old English coin). Sir Thomas, a scrupulous man, commented, *"It would be against good manners to forsake a gentlewoman's New Year gift, and I accept the gloves. The lining you will bestow elsewhere."*

Other types of gloves in the Collection include an interesting group of knitted silk ecclesiastical and secular gloves, mostly Italian and Spanish in origin. The ecclesiastical gloves incorporate knitted Christian symbols in gold thread. The secular examples depict stylized flower and leaf patterns knitted in rich yellows, blues, reds and greens. The earliest pairs of gloves in the Collection are ecclesiastical, deep crimson silk with a gold thread pattern, probably Italian in origin. The Collection also contains samples of fabric gloves, mostly dating from the first half of the 19th century, and printed leather gloves. The latter includes a small group of exquisite Spanish gloves, all wrist-length women's gloves of white kid printed in black with simple geometrical designs or figures from popular engravings.

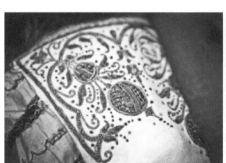

Royal gloves achieves, photo from *Permanent Style*

Her Majesty Queen Elizabeth II's coronation; Glove made by Dents' craftsmen

At each coronation, the ancient symbol of a right-hand glove was presented to the Sovereign by a Peer who had inherited the privilege. A duplicate glove was always made and kept to one side in case any mishap to the original required its use. Those in the Collection are of Queen Victoria, Edward VII, George V, and George VI. Also the collection included the Queen Alexandra's coronation gloves, and the original glove presented to Queen Elizabeth II. The ancient privilege of presenting the glove had lapsed but was revived in 1953 and was transferred to the Glovers Company by the Earl Marshal. The gloves are gauntlet gloves of white leather with a cipher on the back of the hand, and the gauntlets heavily embroidered with gold thread using the traditional motifs of Tudor Rose, the Shamrock, the Thistle, Oak leaves and Acorns.

Grant yourself with an extra-helping hand for fall and winter and experiment with the stylish gloves trend that knows no limits when it comes to fabrics and designs! Vintage-inspired looks, and do not forget about the chic Rock diva outfit essentials, that could be easily complimented with these A-list accessories. Designers managed to cultivated our crave for glove styles and came up with a wide array of long, ruffled, fur, and leather as well as knit gloves in all shades and designs. All you have to do, to raid the stores or go online for the purchase of the chic models!

Traditionally, opera gloves should not be put on in public, but should be donned in the privacy of one's home before going out.

Source: Operagloves.com

Opera gloves are, therefore, properly worn with sleeveless or short-sleeved dresses or strapless, sleeveless (with straps) or short-sleeved evening gowns.

White, and its various shades, including ivory, beige and taupe, are the traditional colors for opera gloves and are appropriate for virtually any occasion on which opera gloves are worn.

Black opera gloves should not be worn with white or light-colored dresses or gowns, but can be worn with black, dark-colored or bright-colored clothing.

Opera gloves of other colors generally should be worn only in coordination with the color scheme of the dress or gown ladies are wearing.

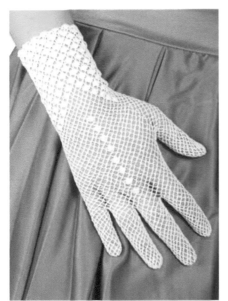

Source: "21st Century Glove Etiquette"

Don't eat, drink or smoke with gloves on.

Don't play cards with gloves on.

Don't apply makeup with gloves on.

Don't wear jewelry over gloves, with the exception of bracelets.

Don't make a habit of carrying your gloves—they should be considered an integral part of your costume.

Don't wear short gloves to a very gala ball, court presentation or "White Tie" affair at the White House or in honor of a celebrity.

Do wear gloves when you go shopping, visiting, driving; and for outdoor festivities such as garden parties and receptions.

Do wear gloves as a mark of respect in a place of worship.

Do wear gloves for formal indoor occasions: receptions, balls, and on arrival at a luncheon or dinner party.

Do keep gloves on in a receiving line.

Do keep gloves on while dancing at a formal party.

Do keep gloves on at a cocktail party until the drinks and hors d'oeurves are passed. Then turn gloves back at the wrist or remove one glove.

Do remove gloves entirely at the dining table.

Do remove gloves after your arrival at an informal party or luncheon, leaving them with your coat.

Source: "Care of Gloves"

1.   Lukewarm water with mild soap flakes, swish gloves and rub fingertips gently.

2.   Put gloves on hands and rinse in clean lukewarm water. Squeeze excess moisture away; some soap will remain on purpose as a softening agent.

3.   Remove gloves and blow into each finger, restoring it to approximate shape. Now, place gloves flat on a towel away from radiator heat, shaping them as you would shape a hand-washed sweater.

4.   When gloves are almost dry, work them—smoothing them on carefully—restoring them to their original shape.

• Cotton and nylon sorties from bright polka-dot prints for the races to embroidered and lace-trimmed fashions for luncheons,

- Black kid for city sightseeing and theater in metropolitan settings,

- String gloves for casual activities in the country or at the beach.

For some people, bridal gloves look tacky. But, please look at the 1950's daytime gloves, with the right outfit and attitude.

Below are polka-dot fishnet gloves with a tiny bow that are incredibly cute! And if you needed some real bride inspiration, look at Jackie Kennedy's wedding style gloves.

Daytime gloves have been part of women's accessories for centuries, but reached its peak in the 1950s. It was customary for a lady to wear short gloves (or "shorties") in the daytime.

"The Etiquette of Opera Gloves" written by Madame Pamela of Maitresse states:

- Your gloves should be kept on when shaking hands (e.g., in a reception line) or when dancing.

- Gloves may also be worn while drinking, though care must be exercised not to spill liquids on them, especially when the gloves are made of kidskin or some other delicate leather. It is better to remove, or partially remove them, when practicable.

- When you sit down to dinner, you should take off your gloves, and put them back on when dinner is over.

- If you remove your opera gloves, you should not take them off in a way that calls undue or seductive attention to the process (unless, of course, you are attempting to seduce the viewer!)

- You can partially remove your opera gloves in this fashion: unbutton the mousquetaire wrist opening and pull your hand out through the opening. The empty glove hand can then be rolled up neatly to wrist level, either tucked under the wrist or under your bracelet, if you are wearing bracelets.

- Six-button (14" or thereabouts) gloves, also known as three-quarter length or coat-length gloves, may properly be worn with just about any length of sleeve. With longer sleeves, the arm-pieces are generally tucked under the sleeves.

- Gauntlet-type gloves (gloves with flared arm-pieces) are also appropriate for wear with most sleeve lengths. The arm-pieces of gauntlets are customarily worn over the sleeve of your blouse or coat.

"When putting on Her gloves, the Lady should work in the hand from the wrist, and then gradually smooth the glove up the arm, rather than pulling from the top. Gloves are worn during the cocktail hour, at least the right glove removed entirely while dining, then worn again for the remainder of the evening (or night!) A Lady does not remove Her glove when shaking hands nor when presenting Her hand to be kissed. It is now very permissible to wear rings and/or a bracelet over one's glove."

"I sometimes smoke on social occasions, but use a cigarette holder to isolate the cigarette from My gloved fingers. Finally, the mousquetaire glove looks much nicer worn buttoned, and I enjoy assigning this difficult, but always pleasurable, task to My escort."

In the Victorian era, it was not exactly proper, as you might imagine, for a lady just to walk up to a gentleman and tell him that she'd like to get to know him better! "Flirtation codes" were developed using a wide variety of objects. The "fan-code" is the best-known, but gloves were also used as flirtation signals. Here are some of the better-known glove signals:

- Twirling one's gloves around her fingers - *We are being watched*
- Holding the tips of the gloves downward - *I wish to be acquainted*
- Gently smoothing the gloves - *I wish I were with you; I would like to talk with you*
- Holding one's gloves loosely in her right hand - *Be contented*
- Holding one's gloves loosely in her left hand - *I am satisfied*
- Striking one's gloves over her hands - *I am displeased*
- Tossing one's gloves up gently - *I am engaged*

- Tapping one's chin with her gloves - *I love another*
- Dropping one of her gloves - *Yes*
- Dropping both gloves - *I love you*
- Turning the wrong side of one's gloves outward - *I hate you*

Of course, many of the above signals involved having to remove at least one glove, which was not considered proper (except at dinnertime, and even then the mousquetaire opening was commonly used to bare the hand and remove the necessity of having to take it all off, so to speak) for opera-length gloves only.

The above information was drawn from "Languages of Love - Museumposten" and "Victorian Gloves and Glove Flirtation" guide.

During the eighteenth century, more accessories had some practical function, but their precise form was dictated by fashion, and sometimes, their design detracted from their usefulness.

The trinity of hats, scarves, and gloves is not only the major set of fashion accessories. Their practical use is to keep our body and soul in healthy order. St. Francis of Assisi said: *"He who works with his hands is a laborer. He who works with his hands and his head is a craftsman. He who works with his hands, his head, and his heart, is an artist."*

Hand knitted with crochet edges fingerless gloves made by Mrs. Ida Tomshinsky

Handmade gloves or mittens make a perfect last-minute gift, since it takes only a few hours to complete. Knitting is more popular today than it has been in decades. Modern day's knitters continue this age-old craft by sprinkling it with their own creativity and individualism. In the end, the ancient craft produces the joy of making something beautiful, and handmade. Knitting and crocheting trends based on a skill, that is a low-tech antidote, survived in a high-tech culture.

Gloves in Literature

According the **Oxford Dictionary,** the definition of glove means "Glove" [OE] Old English **glof** has Germanic origin. From the Middle Ages gloves carried strong social symbolism. Gloves could be used to challenge someone to combat or to confer office. Fine-quality gloves were a sign of status and often given as presents. Expressions *to fit like a glove and hand in glove* both date from the late 18th century, although the latter was in existence earlier as *hand and glove*. The expression *to take the gloves off* meaning 'to use no mercy' dates from the 1920s, although 'to handle without gloves'—the opposite of with *kid gloves* (the softest kind)—date from the early 19th century. The maxim to rule with an *iron fist* or *hand in a velvet glove* has been ascribed to several rulers including Napoleon.

Reference: "Glove" *Oxford Dictionary of Word Origins* by Julia Cresswell. *Oxford Reference Online.* Oxford University Press. ITT Educational Services. 26 November, 2010 2010 <http://www.oxfordreference.com/views/ENTRY. html?subview=Main&entry=t292.e2278>

Curiosities of Literature by Isaac D-Israeli

Curiosities of Literature by Isaac D-Israeli (1766-1848) tells us *The History of Gloves*. The article below is slightly revised from its original in early 1790s editions of the *Curiosities*.

Reference: The present learned and curious dissertation is compiled from the papers of an ingenious antiquary, from the "Present State of the Republic of Letters." Vol. X. P. 289.

The antiquity of this part of dress will form our first inquiry; and we shall then show its various uses in the several ages of the world.

It has been imagined that gloves are noticed in the 108th Psalm, where the royal prophet declares, he will cast his *shoe* over Edom; and still farther back, supposing them to be used in the times of the Judges, Ruth IV. 7, where the custom is noticed of a man taking off his *shoe* and giving it to his neighbor, as a pledge for redeeming or exchanging anything. The word in these two texts usually translated *shoe* By the Chaldean paraphrased in the latter is rendered *glove*. Casaubon is of opinion that *gloves* were worn by the Chaldeans, from the word here mentioned being explained in the Talmud Lexicon, *the clothing of the hand*. But are not these mere conjectures, and has not the Chaldean paraphrased taken a liberty in his version?

Xenophon gives a clear and distinct account of *gloves*. Speaking of the manners of the Persians, as a proof of their effeminacy, he observes, that not satisfied with covering their head and their feet, they also guarded their hands against the cold with *thick gloves. Homer,* describing Laertes at work in his garden, represents him with *gloves on his hands, to secure them from the thorns. Varro,* an ancient writer, has evidence in favor of their antiquity among the Romans. In lib. ii. cap. 55. *de Re Rustica,* he says, that olives gathered by the naked hand are preferable to those gathered with *gloves. Athenæus* speaks of a celebrated glutton who always came to table with *gloves* on his hands, that he might be able to handle and eat the meat while hot, and devour more than the rest of the company.

These authorities show that the ancients were not strangers to the use of *gloves,* though their use was not common. In a hot climate to wear gloves implies a considerable degree of effeminacy. We can more clearly trace the early use of gloves in northern than in southern nations. When the ancient severity of manners declined, the use of *gloves* prevailed among the Romans; but not without some opposition from the philosophers. *Musonius,* a philosopher, who lived at the close of the first century of Christianity, among other invectives against the corruption of the age, says *it is shameful that persons in perfect health should clothe their hands and feet with soft and hairy coverings.* Their convenience, however, soon made the use general. *Pliny,* the younger, informs us, in his account of his uncle's journey to Vesuvius, that his secretary sat by him ready to write down whatever occurred remarkable; and that he had gloves on his hands, that the coldness of the weather might not impede his business.

In the beginning of the ninth century, the use of *gloves* was become so universal, that even the church thought a regulation in that part of dress necessary. In the reign of *Lewis le Debonnaire,* the council of Aix ordered that the monks should only wear *gloves* made of sheepskin.

That time has made alterations in the form of this, as in all other apparel, appears from the old pictures and monuments.

Gloves, beside their original design for a covering of the hand, have been employed on several great and solemn occasions: as in the ceremony of *investitures,* in bestowing lands, or in conferring *dignities*. Giving possession by the delivery of a *glove* prevailed in several parts of Christendom in later ages. In the year 1002, the bishops of Paderborn and Moncerco were put into possession of their sees by receiving a *glove*. It was thought so essential a part of the Episcopal habit that some abbots in France presuming to wear gloves, the council of Poitiers interposed in the affair and forbad them the use, on the same principle as the ring and sandals; these being peculiar to bishops, who frequently wore them richly adorned on their backs with jewels.

Favin observes that the custom of blessing *gloves* at the coronation of the kings of France, which still subsists, is remaining of the eastern practice of investiture by a *glove*. A remarkable instance of this ceremony is recorded. The unfortunate *Conradin* was deprived of his crown and his life by the usurper *Mainfroy*. When having ascended the scaffold, the injured prince lamenting his hard fate, asserted his right to the crown, and as a token of investiture, threw his *glove* among the crowd; entreating it might be conveyed to some of his relations, who would revenge his death. It was taken up by a knight, and brought to Peter, King of Arragon, who in virtue of this glove was afterwards crowned at Palermo.

As the delivery of *gloves* was once a part of the ceremony used in giving possession, so the depriving a person of them was a mark of divesting him of his office, and of degradation. The Earl of Carlisle, in the reign of Edward the Second, impeached of holding a correspondence with the Scots, was condemned to die as a traitor. Walsingham, relating other circumstances of his degradation, says, "His spurs were cut off with a hatchet; and his *gloves* and shoes were taken off, &c."

Another use of *gloves* was in a duel; he who threw one down, was by this act understood to give defiance, and he who took it up, to accept the challenge.

The use of single combat, at first designed only for a trial of innocence, like the ordeals of fire and water, was in succeeding ages practiced for deciding rights and property. Challenging by the *glove* was continued down to the reign of Elizabeth, as appears by an account given by Spelman of a duel appointed to be fought in Tothill Fields, in the year 1571. The dispute was concerning some lands in the county of Kent. The plaintiffs appeared in court, and demanded single combat. One of them threw down his glove, which the other immediately taking up, carried it off on the point of his sword, and the day of fighting was appointed; this affair was however adjusted by the queen's judicious interference.

The ceremony is still practiced of challenging by a *glove* at the coronation of the kings of England, by his majesty's champion entering Westminster Hall completely armed and mounted.

Challenging by the *glove* is still in use in some parts of the world. In Germany, on receiving an affront, to send a *glove* to the offending party is a challenge to a duel.

The last use of *gloves* was for carrying the *hawk,* which is very ancient. In former times, princes and other great men took so much pleasure in carrying the hawk on their hand, that some of them have chosen to be represented in this attitude. There is a monument of Philip the First of France still remaining; on which he is represented at length, on his tomb, holding a *glove* in his hand.

Chambers says that, formerly, judges were forbid to wear *gloves* on the bench. No reason is assigned for this prohibition. Our judges lie under no such restraint; for both they and the rest of the court make no difficulty of receiving *gloves* from the sheriffs, whenever the session or assize concludes without any one receiving sentence of death, which is called a *maiden assize;* a custom of great antiquity.

Our curious antiquary has preserved a singular anecdote concerning *gloves.* Chambers informs us that it is not safe at present to enter the stables of princes without pulling off our gloves. He does not tell us in what the danger consists; but it is an ancient established custom in Germany, that whoever enters the stables of a prince, or great man, with his gloves on his hands, is obliged to forfeit them or redeem them by a fee to the servants. The same custom is observed in some places at the death of the stag; in which case if the *gloves* are not taken off, they are redeemed by money given to the huntsmen and keepers. The French king never failed of pulling off one of his *gloves* on that occasion. The reason of this ceremony seems to be lost.

We meet with the term *glove-money* in our old records; by which is meant money given to servants to buy *gloves.* This probably is the origin of the phrase *giving a pair of gloves,* to signify making a present for some favor or service.

Gough in his "Sepulchral Monuments" informs us that gloves formed no part of the female dress till after the Reformation; I have seen some so late as in Anne's time richly worked and embroidered.

There must exist in the Denny family some of the oldest gloves extant, as appear by the following glove anecdote.

At the sale of the Earl of Arran's goods, April 6th, 1759, the gloves given by Henry VIII to Sir Anthony Denny were sold for 38*l.* 17*s.*; those given by James I. to his son Edward Denny, for 22*l.* 4*s.*; the mittens given by Queen Elizabeth to Sir Edward Denny's lady, 25*l.* 4*s.*; all which were bought for Sir Thomas Denny of Ireland, who was descended in a direct line from the great Sir Anthony Denny, one of the executors of the will of Henry VIII.

A (much) smaller Social History of Ancient Ireland - Chapter XVIII ... Social History of Ancient Ireland - Chapter XVIII - Dress and Personal Adornment. ... "The importance and general use of gloves as an article of dress..." Patrick Weston Joyce - 1903 - History

90, an imaginary personage is spoken of as having "two gloves on his hands"... St. Patrick, when traversing the country in his chariot, wore gloves...

Gloves were commonly worn, and this is proved by many ancient passages and indirect references. They appear to have been common among all classes - poor as well as rich. One of the good works of charity laid down in the Senchus M6r is *"sheltering the miserable,"* which the shiny finish explains, *"to give them staves and gloves and shoes for God's sake."* The evangelist depicted in the **Book of Kells** (p.387) wears gloves, with the fingers divided as in our present gloves, and having the tops lengthened out beyond the natural fingers. Rich people's gloves were often highly ornamented. As to material - probably gloves were made both of cloth and of animal skins and furs. The importance and general use of gloves, as an article of dress, are to some extent indicated by their frequent mention and by the number of names for them. The common word for a glove was *lamann,* which is still in use.

In the 16th and early 17th centuries, it was normal practice, as well as the principle, to fight each other. The traditional situation that led to a duel often happened after the offence. Whether real or imagined, one party would demand satisfaction from the offender. One could signal this demand with an inescapably insulting gesture; such as throwing his glove before him, hence the phrase "throwing down the gauntlet." This originates from medieval times, when a knight was knighted. The knight-to-be would receive the *accolade* of three light blows on the shoulder with a sword and, in some cases, a ritual slap in the face, said to be the last affronts he could accept without redress. Therefore, any one being slapped with a glove was considered—like a knight—obligated to accept the challenge or be dishonored. Contrary to popular belief, hitting one in the face with a glove was not a challenge, but could be done after the glove had been thrown down as a response to the one issuing the challenge.

Illustration: Eugene Onegin and Vladimir Lensky's duel. Pushkin Museum, St. Petersburg

The Russian poet Alexander Pushkin prophetically described a number of duels in his works, notably Onegin's duel with Lensky in *Eugene Onegin*. The poet itself was mortally wounded in a controversial duel with Georges d'Anthès, a French officer rumored to be his wife's lover. D'Anthès, who was accused of cheating in this duel, married Pushkin's sister-in-law and went on to become a French minister and senator.

Dueling began to fall out of favor in America in the 18th century, and the death of former United States Secretary of the Treasury, Alexander Hamilton by dueling—against then the *Vice*

President—did not help its declining popularity. Benjamin Franklin denounced the practice as uselessly violent, and George Washington encouraged his officers to refuse challenges during the American Revolutionary War, because he believed that the death by dueling of officers would have threatened the success of the war effort.

The Scarlet Letter by **Nathaniel Hawthorne:** "A pure hand needs no glove to cover it."

Romeo and Juliet, Act ii. Sc.2 by **William Shakespeare:** "See, how she leans her cheek upon her hand! O that I was a glove upon that hand, that I might touch that cheek!"

Mankind, Man by **Margaret Atwood:** "The basic Female body comes with the following accessories: garter belt, panty-girdle, crinoline, camisole, bustle, brassiere, stomacher, chemise, virgin zone, spike heels, nose ring, veil, kid gloves, fishnet stockings, fichu, bandeau, Merry Widow, weepers, chokers, barrettes, bangles, beads, lorgnette, feather boa, basic black, compact, Lycra stretch one-piece with modesty panel, designer peignoir, flannel nightie, lace teddy, bed, head."

Redburn by **Herman Merville:** "As I was about leaving the forecastle, I happened to look at my hands, and seeing them stained all over of a deep yellow, for the morning the mate had set me to tarring some strips of canvas for the rigging, I thought it would never do to present myself before a gentleman that way; so far want of kids, I slipped on a pair of woolen mittens, which my mother had knit for me to carry to sea…"

The Mitten: A Ukrainian Folk Tale by Jan Brett

The Mitten: A Ukrainian Folk Tale by Jan Brett tells the story of a boy named Nicki whose grandmother knits him a beautiful pair of snow-white mittens. He soon loses one in the snow, and some animals move right in.

More to read: ***The Mitten*** by **Jim Aylesworth**, ***The Mitten*** by **Alvin Tresselt**, ***The Mitten Tree*** by **Candace Christiansen**, etc.

Gloves in Fine Arts: Museum Collections and Displays

It is very common to research objects and their socio-historic aspect through art. Just follow the Wikimedia Commons online in the following Categories: Gloves/Clothing in Art/Culture in Art/Objects in Art/Hands in Art. Any portraits of Frans Hals or Hans Hobbeins will have men and women dressed up and with gloves, where gloves are a part of assemble and dress code status.

"My Fiancé in Black Gloves," 1909 by Marc Chagall

"Stilleben," 1889 by Vincent Van Gogh

Henri Toulouse-Lautrec (1864-1901): "Woman with Gloves" (Honrine P.), c. 1890

Edgar Degas, Fine Art Open Edition Giclée: "Woman Putting on Her Gloves"

Art and design were more closely tied at the turn of the twentieth century. For example, the famed French couturier Paul Poiret demonstrated his artistic sensibilities throughout his career designing costumes' dramas with enrichment of fashion accessories. There is reasonable question: Are fashion and clothing art? Does fashion continue to get inspiration from the world art? The fashion press always employs what influences fashion from street wear to fine arts, TV and movies, and even, modern technology.

Unfortunately, the custom for removing gloves in polite society meant that many portraits do not have the gloves being worn, but held. This makes it more difficult to define the seams and the cut of gloves from visual references only.

Below on the left: London Glove Merchant Charles Smith Sells Lamb-Gloves and Mittens Stretched Canvas Poster Print by Art.com

- Selection of Women's Gloves Including Long White Evening Gloves and Wrist Buttoning Gloves
- Lady Tries on Some Gloves
- French Gloves by Pat Cockerell
- Ladies Gloves in Candy Colors
- Model Modeling Elbow Length Gloves by Nina Leen

Art.com is an online website that offers prints, framed art, and canvas by era and by vintage art, including costume and fashion.

CHARLES SMITH,

At the Crown *and* Glove, *near*
Bow-Church, CHEAPSIDE,
LONDON,

SELLS Men's and Women's Bath Lamb-
Gloves, and Mittins ; and all other Sorts
of Gloves, at Reasonable Rates.

Right: Virginie Amélie Avegno Gautreau,
commonly known as Madame X, in this
John Singer Sargent portrait, painted in 1884

Beside gloves in heraldry, there are royal family members in full fashion parade such as portraits of Mary Tudor by Antonis Mor. The scholars may follow the gateway of females with gloves in art as the Marc Chagall's sexy fiancé in black gloves. Please see the picture above.

Visiting museums, studying portraits, and getting inspiration from fine arts are the key points to any trend sets in art and design, art and fashion. At the current time, women seldom wear opera gloves. The development of the engineering industry with its higher wages attracted the mass production and new standards for quality for any accessories including gloves. Opera gloves now almost vanished, but they are an inspiration for new trend settings.

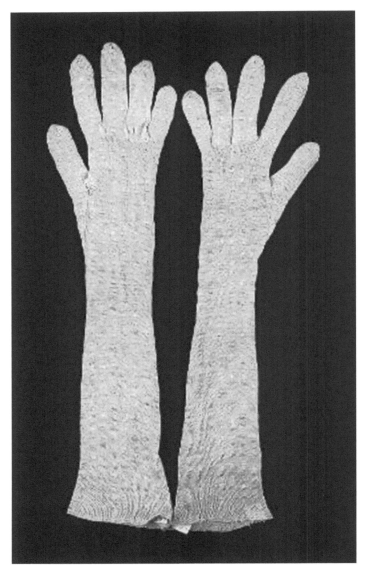

On the left: Long white gloves, plain except three thin bands on top of hand, seam on inside of hand and arm, split in thumb

- American, late 18th to early 19th century

- Place of use: Lexington, Massachusetts, United States

- Place of manufacture: Massachusetts, United States

- Dimensions: 50.5 * 16 cm (19 7/8 * 6 5/16 in.)

- Medium Technique: Hand-knit linen

- Worn by member of Robbins Family; inherited by Ellen A. Stone. Gift to MFA, 1899.

"Pair of Woman's Gloves." Museum of Fine Arts (MFA), Boston

From 15th century, portraits are full of gloves. Due to Lady Katerina da Brescia, a fashion enthusiast, passionate by both history of costume and Florence, the 15th century gloves are shorter in length compare to the medieval times. Colors became more varied and embroidered decorations appeared mainly on the cuffs. During 16th century, the cuffs slowly extend the length and the decorated cuffs became separate from the main pattern. Portraits demonstrate the decorative designs in use such as spangles, lace, embroidery, fringes and jewels. Beside, both men and women would wear heavily decorative gloves. In 17th century, the emphasis was on proper fit, and gloves became less ornamental.

Alexander Roslin

Alexander Roslin

Antoine Pesne Hofdame;
Prinzessin Amalia von
Preussen als Amazone

Bruyn Anne
of Cleves

Carolus-Duran Dame au Gant

Charles Beaubrun María
Teresa de Austria y el
Gran Delfin

Diego Velázquez

Edgar Germain
Hilaire Degas

Eleanor Frances Dixie by
Henry Pickering

Elisabeth-Alexandrine de
Bourbon-Conde de Sens

Ferenczy Ida

Frederick Sandys

Gantsnoirs

Get Fat

Gustave Courbet

Jean Béraud, the
Drinkers

Laszlo - Countess
Ferdinand
Colloredo-Mannsfeld

ML Duchess Parma

Madame de Genlis

Maria Beatrice
Vittoria of Savoy

Maria Isabella di Spagna

Maria Cristina

María Cristina de Borbón

Neyret

Pierre-Auguste Renoir,
la loge (The Theater Box)

Portrait of Woman
with Gloves

Queen Maria

Spirella Service, 1924

Spirella Service, 1924

The Ladies' World March,
1896

Veneto

Veneto

Vigilius Eriksen

Woman Walking Steps in
the Beach

Betty Gleim - Portrait by
Georg Friedrich Adolph
Schöner

"Fashion is art, but art is not always fashion." Perhaps it is true, and it is silly to argue. It is also depends how you look at the piece of art.

Designers and artists are finding new, and sometimes old, materials to work with, and express their point of view. While vintage glove research for potential visual information was attempted, I came across some very inventive creations made from this ladylike accessory. While we may never return to the day when gloves are a required part of a woman's wardrobe, these clever artisans have shown us new uses for them!

Maison Martin Margiela, a designer well known for his innovative perspective in the world of fashion, had designed an original halter top exclusively out of vintage leather evening gloves. It was part of a fashion exhibit held back in 2007.

Dolce & Gabbana had models walking in their Fall 2009 show with leather gloves as fascinators. This was certainly a show stopping eccentric look that had milliners everywhere stop and take notice.

Louise Black is another designer who took the gloves off to design black and white corset out of vintage gloves. She tells, *"I'd had the gloves for a while, bought the entire log of vintage accessories at an estate sale. I was watching the movie "Beetle Juice" while exercising one night and liked the way Delia Deetz was wearing a glove on her arm and some in her hair. I started thinking it would be neat to work those gloves, I'd been hanging onto, into an outfit. Also I needed to do something special for my project runway audition, thus was born the glove corset."*

"100 Gloves" project by Terry Towery evolved in real time on Facebook. *"My Facebook "friends" got to watch as images were added irregularly. An arbitrary set of conditions governed the project."* The "rules" as the [Terry Towery] set them out were:

a. all gloves must be found in situ, no altering the scene allowed,
b. the gloves were left in place,
c. natural available light only,
d. iPhone camera only.

"One thing is an object, two things are a pair. Three make a collection, and 100 things become art," – *said* Robert Rindler, Dean of the School of Art at Cooper Union, in the review to the "100 Gloves" project.

Jo Ann Callis is an artist and a photographer. Since she emerged in the late 1970s as one of the first important practitioners of the "fabricated photographs" movement, Jo Ann Callis has made adventurous contributions in the areas of color photography, sculpture, painting, and digital imagery. For her, photography is another studio tool to be used, along with the sets she creates, and the models she directs,

Glove, Balloon, Shoehorn, 1983
All images © Jo Ann Callis

to render the sensual tones and textures of fabric and food, or to animate clay figures of her own making. The persistent inventiveness of Callis's work has made her a force in Southern California Art and in recent photographic practice. Collis refers to the group of combined black-and-white still life studies she made in 1982–83 as *The Grid* series.

She started with familiar household objects that, individually, gave her comfort. She selected the adjacencies with care and added strong, focused overhead lighting, intending to create a sort of drama, or imagined conversation, between the objects. The resulting assemblages cause the viewer to give common objects new importance and, perhaps, new meaning.

Harley Jo Harrison from Ohio State University graduated from College of the Arts with BFA with honors and created the surrealistic painting aka Salvadore Dali to emphasize the fashion accessories in the portrait below.

This original painting brings together incongruous and unrelated objects: the head of a classical Greek statue, an oversized rubber glove, a green ball, and a train shrouded in darkness, silhouetted against a bright blue sky. By subverting the logical presence of objects, de Chirico created what he termed "metaphysical" paintings, representations of what lies "beyond the physical" world. Cloaked in an atmosphere of anxiety and melancholy, de Chirico's humanoid forms, vacuous architecture, shadowy passages, and inharmoniously elongated streets evoke the profound absurdity of a universe torn apart by World War I.

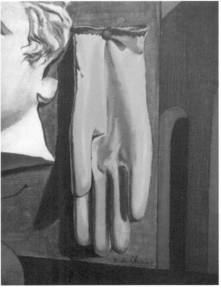

(On Left) "Assignment 2: Vogue" by Harley Jo Harrison

(On Right) Fragment from The Song of Love Paris, June-July 1914
Oil on canvas, 28 3/4 x 23 3/8"
(73 x 59.1 cm) Giorgio de Chirico (Italian, born Greece, 1888-1978)

A unique and original impression of "Glove Display" by Susan Hall has been hand-colored with watercolor, and then given a specific number. The "Glove Display" is marked 'AP #08, meaning the eighth Artist Proof impression. Because the work involved individual impressions, each of her prints is clearly a work of art. The images by Susan Hall are protected by copyrights.

- The artist biography, research and information pertaining to her original work of art has been written and designed by Greg & Connie Peters, exclusively for www.artoftheprint.com.

Textile artist, Rachel Denny Wright, designed a rug or wall hanging out of vintage gloves for DesignMilk.com. Rachel Denny works in a variety of materials - wood, plaster, resin, wool, found objects - to name a few. She is continually excited by the potential of her materials, and how they can be manipulated in unexpected ways. *"I am inspired by the elegant forms found in the natural world and the time honored action of trying to depict these forms in a relevant and interesting way that is homage to this beauty and wonder."*

Fashion and artwork always blend designers and retailers' showcases with their wares alongside with fine artifacts. Remember Madonna's fingerless lace gloves or Michael Jackson's crystal studded white glove of the 1980's? Michael Jackson would wear a single glove on one hand leaving the other hand gloveless.

King of Pop is known for his lavish and frivolous spending sprees. The most persuasive and intriguing symbol of celebrity during the modern time is that of a piece of decorative wearing apparel - Michael Jackson's single white glove. Since Jackson himself no longer wears the item, as far as one can tell, he made something of a "vow" effect of pop culture.

Today, it became as a piece of cultural archeology within past history. Apparently, as the story goes, Michael Jackson planned to liquidate approximately 2,000 of his possessions in a public auction, including gloves. The auction was to be conducted by Julien's Auctions. It became as a point of big controversy. Jackson's MJJ Productions stopped the sale from moving forward and contended that the items are being sold without Michael Jackson's permission. Later, *Reuters* reported that the auction, originally planned was officially cancelled, and possessions were returned to Michael Jackson.

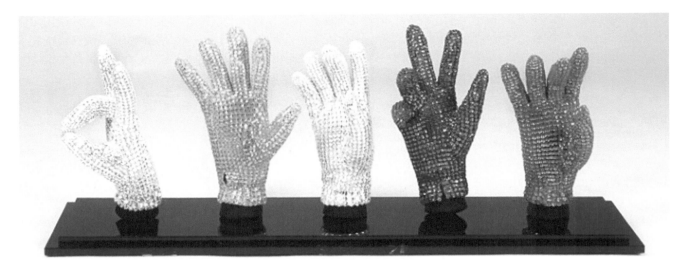

Michael's signature gloves covered in Swarovski loch spark crystals - worth £4,000 to £4,500

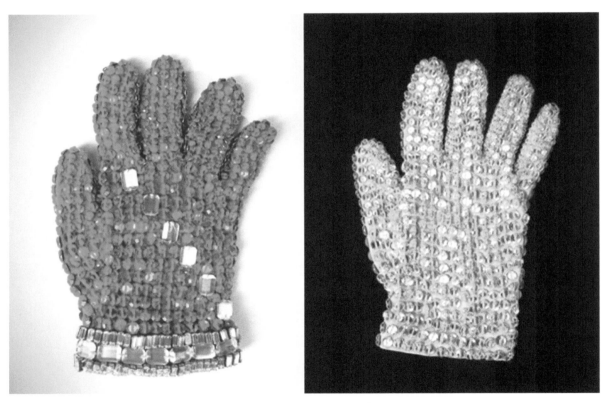

Treasures from Neverland

Ever wonder where Mickey and Minnie's gloves came from? Apparently, main reason for adding the white gloves was to allow audiences see their hands when they were against their bodies, since their skin was black. Mickey did not appear in color until 1935. The three black lines on the back of the gloves are fabric darts extending from between the digits of the hand, which was typical of kid glove designs of the time.

There is a growing trend in our subculture to make cakes and cap cakes by creating eatable objects as food, and in the end, presenting the Culinary art's exhibits for mass production.

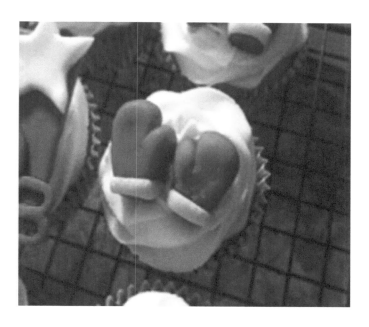

Culinary art: winter mittens on a cap cake

Victorian Tea Parties

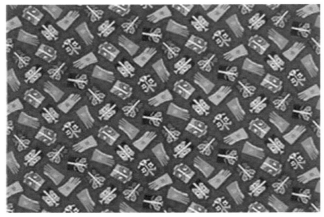

Cowboy Shirts and Gloves on Blue Cotton Fabric
Nancy's Fabrics online shop - $6.99

Red Hat Flannel Gloves Purses Cotton Fabric- $5.99

http://www.nancysfabrics.com/product/cowboy-shirts-and-gloves-on-blue-cotton-fabric

Chicago artist Ellen Greene represents the focal point that showcases of modern discoveries in fashion, music, photography, art and pop culture. Ellen Greene makes leather gloves with 'tattoos' on them. She paints old-school sailor tattoos onto them. Those Swiss lambskin military pieces in Paris [2011] were sensational. The fashion brand of Jack Spade created a new concept in winter fashion: the moustache gloves. Available in red, blue, and grey and yellow, they are recommended for putting right below your nose.

These designers do not see the difference between creating an original work of art wear, and designed a textile pattern that would be reproduced many times over. Each is a valid creative act in their eyes.

Christopher Guests' character, in the 1987 Rob Reiner film *The Princess Bride*, wears a six-fingered glove as his villainous character The Six-Fingered Man. The 1980s horror film series *Nightmare on Elm Street* also produced a famous gloved villain in Freddy Kruger. Kruger wore an unforgettable glove that gave the illusion that he had knives for fingers.

White Gloves Woven Contemporary Tapestry | 46"x53"

Feminine beauty, bold colors and fashion statements characterize the *Vogue* inspiration for tapestries. Complementing a bold décor, the *Vogue* tapestries will create a stir and a conversation in any home. Woven on jacquard looms and made in USA. True tapestries are woven works of art. All of the wall tapestries are woven on jacquard looms and utilize between nine and seventeen miles of thread in each design. The color palates of the warp and weft threads work in concept to achieve a broad range of colors on the face of the tapestry. Tapestries have texture not found in any other art form. The combination of the treads and waves creates a unique art experience that changes with each viewing angle.

Here is another example of artistic use the ancient fashion accessory in animation. *"My initial interest was to explore a number of themes for films which could be part of a small collection of animations for inclusion in an animated cabinet of curiosities. Each film would be based on ideas developed from a single object and its stories or associations,"* said Jo Lawrence, an artist in residence, in the online blog. Originally, she got inspired after a visit to the Dents factory and Museum in Warminster and translated the inspiration into a storyboard for a movie. Jo Lawrence writes in her blog, *"My intention before I leave the studio in two weeks is to make various props for the film, including one giant glove 4 meters high, resolve Glover's mask, make a few reptilian gloves and a world map which shows the edge of the world."*

Jo Lawrence's movie "Glover" inspired by her visit to Dents' factory in Warminster

Glover's story was inspired by the fusion of two sources of inspiration from the V&A's vast collection: a reproduction of the Ebstorf Map and a pair of ornate leather and satin gloves (1600). The Ebstorf map is a representation of the medieval view of the world in 1300. The 'glove-creatures' in Glover's interior world are a departure from the familiar, known and safe world of his workshop. Glover's journey takes him to the furthest reaches of his imagination, Terra Chirotheca, or Gloveland. It is a place of, horror and delight in the same time, where he meets a series of strange hybrids that are part beast and human, and part glove. "Glover" has been shortlisted for the Short Film category of the British Animation Awards 2010, and selected for the Public Choice Award. It was screened at twenty-seven venues across the United Kingdom during 2010.

The classic photography brings us to unforgettable images of Irvin Penn and Cecil Beaton. The "Balenciaga's Gathered Sleeve, 1950" taken by Irvin Penn is on the edge images of both high fashion and high level of photography. Sir Cecil Beaton's "Greta Garbo, 1946" demonstrates the gold standard of the glove as fashion accessory. Irvin Penn, Sir Cecil Beaton, Horst, Edward Steichen, the pioneers of fashion photography, helped to preserve the images of gloves in fashion as a staple of elegance and vogue.

The 20th century marked the beginning of an enlarged understanding of fashion as an art form moving these attitudes into 21st century.

The picture contains *latex gloves* for cleaning and cooking displayed in an unusual way that makes the picture interesting.
Posted by Dawn, co-founder of Rouxbe blog, c.2007

Bibliography

A few tomes that give us real insight of early gloves. One of the more revered in existence today is *Le Gant*. The book, while entirely in French, reveals many patterns and divulges a brief development and history of the glove.

Much of the information about the history of opera gloves from Josephine to Shania was drawn from C. Cody Collins' 1945 book, *Love of a Glove* (Fairchild). This little book, unhappily long out of print, is a veritable goldmine of information on gloves. Other sources of information used in this article include *Gloves*, Valerie Cumming (Anchor Press, 1982); *Hand In Glove*, Bill Severn (David McKay, 1965); and *Gloves Past and Present*, Willard M. Smith (Imperial, 1918). All these books are out of print but can be found in well-stocked public libraries.

The *Costume Ring* site that is owned by Franchesca V. Havas offers a list of books that are not available for sale and also are out of print, but are available in the library collections and could be received throughout the Interlibrary Loans (IL). The list below includes resources from bibliography by Gail A. Lifkowitz, glove enthusiast.

- Anderson, Ruth Matilda
  Hispanic Costume 1480 - 1530. New York, 1979. Figures 210-214, 514-516. pp 30, 79, 83, 85-86, 115, 222-223, 247. New York: Hispanic Society, 1951. Small 4 to. 334 pp., 392 illus.

- Arnold, Janet
  Queen Elizabeth's Wardrobe Unlocked. – Leeds: Maney, 1988.

- Beck, S. William
  Gloves, Their Annals and Associations. Hamilton, Adams & Co., London, 1883. -Detroit: Singing Tree Press, 1969.

- Boehn, Max von
  Ornament, Supplement to Modes and Manners. Benjamin Blom Inc., 1929, reissued 1970. pp 68-93.

- Close, Eunice.
  How to Make Gloves. -Boston: Charles T. Branford Co., 1950.

- **Museum of Costume**, "Gloves for Favors, Gifts, and Coronations, Elizabeth I - Elizabeth II." Handout of exhibit, Bath, England, 1988.

- Cumming, Valerie.
  Gloves. Accessories of Dress series. – London: Batsford Ltd, 1982.

- Cunnington, Phyllis.
  Handbook of English Costume in the 16th Century. – Great Britain: Plays, Inc., 1970, pp 50, 143-5, 182-3.

- Digby, George Wingfield. **Elizabethan Embroidery.**

- Ellis, B. Eldred.
  Gloves and the Glove Trade. –London: Sir Isaac Pitman & Sons Ltd, 1921.

- **Encyclopaedia Britannica, Inc.** The History of Gloves. Handout R. – 1976. - 7 pages.

- Faulkner-Wagner, Jan,
  "Handmaking Leather Gloves." – *Threads*, #19, Oct/Nov., 1988.

- Foster, Vanda.
  "A Garden of Flowers" [A note of some unusual embroidered gloves.] –*Costume,* #14, 1980.

- Garofalo, Cara.
  "A Glove Museum Extends a Hand to the Past." - *Victoria Magazine*, October, 1994, pp. 34-36.

- Hummel, Edith M.
  You Can Make Your Own Gloves: 2nd/ed. –New York: Fairchild Publications Inc., 1950.

- Latour, A.
  Ciba Review #61. October, 1947.Ciba (Latour): 061 GLOVES The Glove, a Badge of Office. Glove-making Centres. Glove Manufacture. Modish Changes in Glove Fashions; 1947 (52) CIBA REVIEWS 1937-1974 facsimile 950. Offered for sale by Myrna Bloom, The EAST-WEST ROOM

- Lester, Katherine Morris.
  An Illustrated History of Accessories of Dress. – Peoria, IL: Manual Arts Press, 1940, pp 354-367.

- Lopez, R. S. & Raymond, I. W.
  Medieval Trade in the Mediterranean World. –New York, 1955, pp 56-60. (reference in "Early Medieval Kingship" by Sawyer and Wood, University of Leeds, 1977)

There are also extensive period gloves to be found in books on period embroidery and costume accessories. The list below includes resources selected by Ida Tomshinsky, the "Fashion Librarian" and glove enthusiast.

The majority of books on this list could be purchased at www.amazon.com such as **Hats, Gloves, Scarves: Easy Designer Knits for Family and Friends** [Paperback] by Louisa Harding

1. **100 Gloves** by Terry Towery. – 1989.

2. **A History of Costume** by Carl A. Kohler.

3. **Cables: Mittens, Hats & Scarves (Vogue Knitting on the Go!)** by Trisha Malcolm, Carla S. Scott, and Tanis Gray (Editor). – 2008

4. *Carolina Amato*: **From Hand to Head** by Jill Newman.–"WWD," 24 August, 1990

5. **Colorwork Creation: 30+ Patterns to Knit Gorgeous Hats, Mittens and Gloves** by Susan Anderson-Freed

6. **Crafts of the North American Indians: A Craftsman's Manual.** (pp. 95-104). Written, illustrated & published by Richard C. Schneider. – 1972

7. **Folk Knitting in Estonia: A Garland of Symbolism, Tradition and Technique (Folk Knitting Series)** by Nancy Bush. - 2000

8. **Folk Style: Innovative Designs to Knit, Including Sweaters, Hats, Scarves, Gloves and More (Style Series)** by Mags Kandis. – 2007

9. **Forgotten Fashion: An Illustrated Faux History of Outrageous Trends and Their Untimely Demise** by Kate Hahn. – 2008

10. **Glove Knitting** by Nanette Blanchard. – 2009

11. **Glove Making: The Art and Craft** by Gwen Emlyn-Jones. -1974

12. *Gloves* by Marie de Lyon Lochac. – "A & S" Supplement Issue #2, Dec.

13. **Gloves, Fashion & Etiquette** by Edith Heal. - 1961

14. **Gloves: Their Annuals and Associations: A Chapter of Trade and Social History (1883)** by S. William Beck. – 2007

15. **Gloves: Vintage Crochet Patterns for 1950s Style** by J. & P. Coats. – 2009

16. **Happy Gloves: Charming Softy Fiends Made from Colorful Gloves** by Miyako Kanamori. – 2008

17. **Hats, Gloves, Scarves: Easy Designer Knits for Family and Friends** by Louisa Harding. – 2005

18. **Head to Toe Knits: 35 Hats, Scarves, Gloves and Socks You'll Love to Knit** by Brownyn Lowenthal and Melody Griffiths. - 2010

19. **Homespun, Handknit: Caps, Socks, Mittens & Gloves** by Linda Ligon. -1988

20. **Knitting Fair Isle Mittens and Gloves: 40 Great-Looking Designs** by Carol Rasmussen Noble and Carol Noble. – 2002

21. **Knitting New Mittens and Gloves: Warm and Adorn Your Hands in 28 Innovative Ways** by Robin Melanson and Tyllie Barbosa. – 2008

22. **Ladies' Vintage Accessories** by LaRee Johnson Bruton. - 2000

23. **Latvian Mittens: Traditional Design & Techniques** by Lizbeth Upitis. – 1997

24. **Love of a Glove: The Romance, Legends, and Fashion History of Gloves (How to Know Gloves and How They are Made).** - 1947

25. **Magnificent Mittens & Socks: The Beauty of Warm Hands and Feet** by Anna Zilboorg and Alexis Xenakis. – 2010

26. **Make Your Own Gloves** by Gwen Emlyn-Jones. – 1975

27. **Mostly Mittens: Ethnic Knitting Designs from Russia** by Charlene Schurch. – 2009

28. **On the Edge Images from 100 Years of "Vogue."**

29. **Paris Sponsors Crochet: Vintage Patterns for 1930s Hats, Gloves, Belts and Collars (Book 66)** by Spool Cotton Co. – 2009

30. **Practical Glove Making** by Isabel M. Edwards. - 2009

31. **Queen Elizabeth's Wardrobe Unlock'd** by Janet Arnold –1988

32. **Royal and Historic Gloves and Shoes** by W. B. Redfern. -2009

33. **Shoes, Hats and Fashion Accessories: A Pictorial Archive, 1850-1940** by Carol Belanger Grafton.

34. **Sock and Glove: Creating Charming Softy Friends from Cast-off Socks and Gloves** by Miyako Kanamori. – 2007

35. **Socks-Gloves and Mittens Fashion in Wool (Volume 52)** by Hilde. – 1946

36. **Stitch Style Mittens: Twenty Fashion Knit and Crochet Styles** by Michell Lo. – 2007

37. **The Art of Embroidery** by Marie Schuette and Sigrid Muller-Christensen. – London: Thames and Hudson, 1964.

38. **The Glove Cities: How a People and Their Craft Built Two Cities: A Sociological and Economic History of the Glove and Glove Leather Indu** by Barbara McMartin (April 1999)

39. **The 2009-2014 Outlook for Leather Gloves and Mittens in India** by Icon Group. -2009

40. **The 2009-2014 World Outlook for Leather-and-Fabric Gloves and Mittens Made from Purchased Leather and Fabrics** by Icon Group. - 2008

41. **The 2009-2014 World Outlook for Manufacturing Cut and Sew Gloves and Mittens** by Icon Group. – 2008

42. ***Treasures from Neverland*** by Paul Toscano. – "Reuters", 10 March, 2009. Updated 15 April 2009.

43. **Vogue Knitting Mittens & Gloves (Vogue Knitting on the Go)** by Trisha Malcolm. -2003

44. **Vogue Knitting Mittens & Gloves** by Editors of Vogue Knitting Magazine. -2010

45. **Weekend Knitting: 50 Unique Projects and Ideas** by Melanie Falick. -2003

46. ***Well in Hand.*** – "Handmade magazine," Winter 1990, p. 86.

47. **What Every Member of the Trade Community Should Know About [Electronic Resource]: Gloves. Mittens, Mitts, Not Knitted or Crochet, Under the HTSUS** by U.S. Customs and Border Protection. – [2006]

48. **Women's Norwegian Mittens - A Vintage Knitting Pattern for Kindle!** by Northern Lights Vintage. – 2009 (Kindle eBook)

49. **You Can Make Your Own Gloves** by Edith M. Hummel. -194?

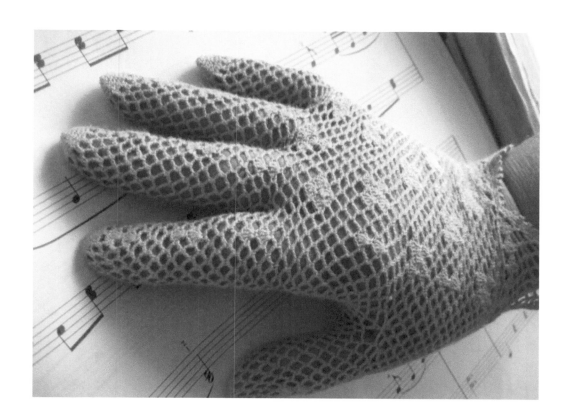

Webliography

1. http://carolinaamato.com

2. http://en.wikipedia.org/wiki/Evening_glove (Retrieved 2010-16-11)

3. http://dents.co.uk/documents/dents-brocure.pdf

4. http://pernamentstyle.co.uk/2010/dents-how-btitish-gloves-are-made.html

5. http://www.articlealley.com/article_22386_34.html?ktrack=kcplink

6. http://www.familyforest.info/gloves.htm

7. http://www.goantiques.com/scripts/images,id,734503.html – Cosmopolitan Magazine, 5/49. Cover is Gloves by Merry Hull. 196 pages

8. http://www.MillionLooks.com

9. Edgar Degas Fine Art Open Edition Giclée:"Woman Putting on Her Gloves" - Museum Collections http://www.gallerydirectart.com/ged-66208.html?utm_source=Froogle&utm_medium=Shopping%2BPortal&utm_term=ged-66208&utm_campaign=Shopping%2BPortal#ixzz18JmLjLvd (GalleryDirectArt.com 1-800-733-1144)

10. "Fall 2010 Accessories Trend: Endless Gloves" by Roxanne Robinson-Escriout. –wwd.com, March 22, 2010

11. "For the Love of Opera Gloves." http://operagloves.com/glovmain.html (Retrieved 2010-19-11)

12. "Glove." Encyclopedia Britannica. 2010. Encyclopedia Britannica Online. 08 Dec. 2010 <http://www.britannica.com/EBchecked/topic/235748/glove>

13. Glove enthusiast, Taylor Hartley, conducts and posts research regarding all types of gloves. For more information regarding industrial and personal use gloves, visit http://www.unitedglove.com

14. "Gloves." http://www.pbm.com/~lindahl/rialto/clothing_book-msg.html

15. Gloves and muffs. Making gloves. http://www.florilegium.org/files/ACCESS/gloves-msg.html

16. "Gloves - Fashion, Costume, and Culture: Clothing, Headwear, Body Decorations, and Footwear through the Ages." http://www.fashionencyclopedia.com/fashion_costume_culture/Early-Cultures-Europe-in-the-Middle-Ages/Gloves.html#ixzz19pwPOPFa

17. "How to Make Gloves." http://www.glove.org

18. "La Mode Francaise: Historical Note on Gloves." http://www.lamodefrancaise.tm.fr/anglais/culture/historiques/gants.htm

19. Latvian Education Information System, "Ritms un simetrija Latviešu cimdu rakstos," http://www.liis.lv/cimdi/frame1.htm

20. Links to info on medieval gloves and mittens by Dame Aoife Finn of Ynos Mon. http://www.florilegium.org/files/ACCESS/glovs-mittns-lnks.html

21. Mowbray, Nicole. (2004-04-04). "Japanese girls choose whiter shade of pale". London: Guardian Unlimited. http://www.guardian.co.uk/japan/story/0,7369,1185335,00.html. Retrieved 2010-05-02

22. "The Gloves of Fulton County: A Documentary Video." http://www.albany.edu/history/histmedia/glove_documentary/Glove_doc_video.html

23. "The History of the Opera Glove." http://operagloves.com/history.html

24. "The Renaissance Tailor." http://www.vertetsable.com/demos_gloves.htm

25. Unique Arm Warmers Have Taken the World by Storm (http://www.capetown partnership.co.za/unique-arm-warmers-have-taken-the-world-by-storm/)." Cape Town Partnership. Retrieved on July 5, 2010.

26. World Federation of Free Latvians. "Latviešu ornamentu pamatelementi un to nozīme (simboli)," http://www.pbla.lv/izglitiba/ornamenti.htm

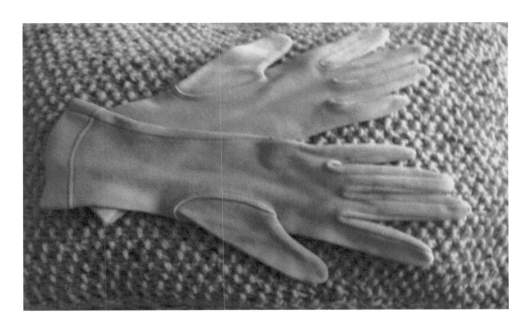